"Unlike Roy Bhaskar's writing style, his lectures were very clear and listener-friendly. Fortunately, Gary Hawke recorded some of Roy Bhaskar's final lectures, and has edited them into this excellent book, valuable both for beginners and for more experienced critical realists."

Priscilla Alderson, Professor Emerita, University College London Institute of Education

The Order of Natural Necessity

Natural Necessity is the state or truth of what things are and the causal power that they have to affect the world.

Natural Necessity means that a thing has no alternative but to act in the way it does. This can be as simple as a smile when we hear a funny joke, a tear when we feel sadness, to the global destruction of our planet due to global warming.

The Natural Necessity of things is their causal power, however, causal powers can be realised, or un-realised.

The Order of Natural Necessity works towards the creation of a transformational imagination; in which together we can create a world where causal powers that limit freedom are blocked, and the causal powers that allow the flourishing of freedom, love, and wellbeing for all are realised.

Title: The Order of Natural Necessity: A Kind of Introduction to Critical Realism/Roy Bhaskar; edited with a preface by Gary Hawke.

Cover design by Gary Hawke – Fractal image PeteLinforth.
Back Cover Quote - Bhaskar (2002/2012a: 304)
Typeset in Bembo by Gary Hawke, UK
Transcription by Anne Hewitson

As editor Gary Hawke undertook this project, from text, to illustrations, to footnotes to book design. If you do find a typo, please contact Gary at garyhawke.org@gmail.com

ISBN-13: 978-1537546827
ISBN-10: 1537546821
BISAC: Philosophy / General

The Order of Natural Necessity

A Kind of Introduction to Critical Realism

By

Professor Roy Bhaskar

Edited and with a Preface by Gary Hawke

Based on "An Introduction to Critical Realism", a series of virtual talks hosted by Gary Hawke and given by Professor Roy Bhaskar at the University College London: Institute of Education

May to July 2014

Contents

The Order of Natural Necessity

Figures

Tables

"As a philosopher ... I have never felt totally happy ... I am not sure what my complete dharma or what my dharma conceived as itself evolving really is."...

Roy Bhaskar (2010: 21) The Formation of Critical Realism

Foreword

Gary Hawke

For 10 years I have, as a dramatherapist, run workshops and retreats that one could call spiritual, or transpersonal. The aim of my work is to assist the experience of non-duality. However, my greatest frustration was when the west took the eastern spiritual tradition concept of non-duality and spoke of it as being an awakening experience or an experience of enlightenment that you either experienced spontaneously or worked hard to experience.

This idea of spontaneously vs. hard work made little sense to me; if, I argued, at an ontological level, there is freedom, all we need to do is take away the blocks to the experience of that freedom. However, in 2011 I was fortunate to hear Roy Bhaskar the originator of Critical Realism speaking on what it means to be an activist of the real. Although I could see that Roy was offering some very complex philosophical ideas, he was also offering them in a way that was clear, understandable, and for me inspiring.

I was profoundly struck by his simple idea that non-duality is not a mystical metaphysical concept that we work hard to achieve, or just awaken to, it is the very causal power what allows society to interact, it is the meta-level, or cosmic envelope, without which you and I would not be able to understand each other as embodied personalities.

I was, and I still am, overwhelmed by Roy's simple explanation of the non-dual. It has changed my work, my ideas, and my view of what true or alethic freedom is.

This book's beginning comes from an ending. In 2014, after much persuasion, I managed to get Roy in front of a computer in the University College London - Institute of Education's library ready to start a series of live streamed talks of what was to become six hours of Roy talking about critical realism.

After my original introduction to Roy's philosophy of metaReality (see chapter three) I contacted Roy, as I wanted to explore the unpublished volume four of the philosophy of metaReality: The Workins. MetaReality states that if we want emancipation from occlusions we need to work on the blocks, just as we work out in the gym, we should work in, to explore our own embodied personality and look to how one creates a deeper finer connection to the non-dual, which is at the heart of the metaReal.

I also wanted to know more of the other stages in the development of critical realism, and so I began what was to become an uphill struggle to penetrate Roy's, at times, dense academic texts. I managed to gain enough understanding of critical realism to be able to introduce some of Roy's idea on human emancipation and wellbeing into my dramatherapy and therapeutic coaching work, enough to be able to present my work at the 2013 International Conference for Critical

Realism, a presentation that Roy attended and from which he invited me to join his critical realism reading group at the Institute for Education based in London.

It was listening to Roy speaking at the reading group that I began to think about the possibility of recording Roy. I felt that if I could get Roy just to speak about his work it would open up his philosophy to more people. Therefore, along with my friend Donald Clark we planned to get Roy online.

There are pages I can write about the difficulty Donald and I encountered, from not being able to use certain online tools, to having to move streaming times around because of the 2014 Football World Cup. However, in the end we managed to stream Roy live, record Roy, and upload the videos to YouTube. This was the first part of our plan. The second part was the creation of live, streamed, and recorded seminars with Roy, both to help promote his work and to develop an income for Roy. Then, in late 2014 we heard the sad news that Roy had died.

Donald and I then began to consider the possibility of creating a book based on the videos we had of Roy speaking. The aim of the book would be to keep it simple or as simple as possible, changing very little of Roy's spoken words, adding footnotes that aimed to expand the text and understanding, along with introducing the reader to the wider literature on critical realism.

Roy set out to show that we must not ignore what is real, and what is real or alethic real is freedom, we all have within ourselves a connection to freedom, we have just lost that connection.

I did not want Roy's ideas on freedom to become a footnote; to be seen as an academic that had much to say, but said it in a way that was too difficult or too time consuming to understand. With his passing, I did not want him to become a dead academic. I wanted his words to live, to inspire, and to support change in the world.

This book concludes, and realises a promise I made to Roy, that I would ensure that as many people as possible would hear Roy speaking. In keeping to that promise, I have spent 18 months editing this book.

It is the order of my natural necessity to make this book available, not just as a kind of introduction to critical realism but also as the voice of a man who put others before himself. Roy asked deep and challenging questions about the world, seeking to provide a way out of enslavement and in his ideas reached for liberation, but then he stops short and asks:

How are you going to take up the universal project of emancipation that is at the heart of your own order of natural necessity?

Your free flourishing is a condition of the free flourishing of all; this is The Order of Natural Necessity.

Critical Realism in Just Under a 1000 Words

As part of the development of this book I was asked to write a short introduction to critical realism without using or at least with the fewest critical realism terms. This is what I produced. I am offering the text here to show that critical realism, as a philosophical position does not need to be difficult in the telling.

In just under 1000 words, I am going to try to introduce critical realism. I am going to cut corners and generalise, but I hope that I have explained with some seriousness what critical realism is all about.

To read these words, you have to perceive them. Through your perception or senses, you are then judging the words and because you and I speak the same language, your judgements lead to informed interpretations. Even if I spoke in a language that you did not understand, this would only be an interpretive issue and you could just go and get a translation.

It is this process of **Sense>Judge>Interpret** that allows you and I to understand the world. It is also the same process that is used to support the thinking that reality is something we create, or that reality is all in how we come to **Sense>Judge>Interpret** the world, a process known as Epistemology, or the study of what is known, and Empirical or deriving information from our senses.

The famous philosopher David Hume believed that this was how we came to know the world. It was only in our interpretations that we saw that things appeared to affect things. Therefore, when a snooker ball hits another snooker ball it is only in our imagined interpretation that we know that the second hit snooker ball will move. Alternatively, that because there was a sunrise today, there will be a sunrise tomorrow.

Although we might now read this as complete nonsense, it was not really until another famous philosopher called Immanuel Kant came along to challenge Hume's claims did we start to question what was really real. Kant suggested that there is the reality that we create from interpretive data of the objects that we sense and judge. He called this the realm of phenomena. Then, there is the real object or the thing-in-itself, which exists in the realm of noumenon - the realm in which the real thing exists beyond our sensing of it. Kant said that, okay, we know that it is out there, but it is beyond the mind and therefore is not knowable.

Although this appears to sound better than Hume, it still says that there is a real world out there that we can never know and leaves the idea of creating our own reality still the main direction of most of western philosophy. However, what would we have to do if we wanted to change direction and start to think the unthinkable, if we wanted to know the real, how might we proceed?

We might ask a question that goes something like this: "What kind of things exist that form the referent that I am sensing?" The referent is the thing that we are referring to when we create sensory information; it is the disgrace of postmodernism in how it removed the things we refer to when we begin to think about the world. Without things to refer to, we only have interpretation, meaning your interpretation is just as good as mine, so all interpretations are relative and no interpretation is wrong.

Meaning, if we truly want to know and explore Kant's noumenon as a knowable domain, we have to extend our model to include the thing we are referring to; that means we need to add the referent to our model, which now looks like this:

Referent>Sense>Judge>Interpret

If we go back to my illustration about words, we might now begin to think what kinds of things need to exist for my words to appear as sensory information. We are now looking for the supporting mechanisms that bring my words into existence. This starts to get very complex because we could think about Gary and how he is trying to find the best way of explaining something that he has spent many years thinking about, which we might term the Psychological/Philosophical Level. We could explore the Natural Level: the way in which the brain processes information or how Gary is physically shaped. We might explore the way that we interpret information such as shared language or class upbringing; this all would be the Cultural/Social Level. We might think about the process of writing and reading, such as schooling, economic factors, or construction of materials, along with political factors in that Gary has freedom to say what he likes, we could also consider religion, as it is possible that Gary is saying something that is anti-religious, which would be the Material/Systems Level. We could call this process of exploring levels as Ontology or the study of what things exist.

All these mechanisms help generate my words, and not just my words but also everyone's words. These mechanisms make up the words as thing-in-itself, independent of our senses.

Now we have started to explore some universal elements that are the same for all word construction. Therefore, before you sense my words, you refer to the things that generate the possibility of my words, and because those possibilities are the possibilities for all words, we have collapsed that our interpretations create reality. We are able to arrive at the conclusion that there is a world that is independent of our senses that has an actual expression, which we come to know through our senses. There are generative mechanisms that allow Gary's words to exist, (which the reader may know or not know about) which appear as dots on a screen or marks on paper which through sensing and judging the reader interprets.

This is critical realism: the proposal that there are **(The) Real** universal generative mechanisms out in the world that we may or may not know about, sense or not sense. That these mechanisms create the possibility of an **(The) Actual** event, from which we interpret as **(The) Empirical** data, in our own unique way, never forgetting that we are only seeing a very small part of a very big real world we are part of.

The Structure of the Book

In the original live streaming, over the course of three two-hour talks, Roy explored and explained the three main stages of critical realism. The aim of the talks was to introduce critical realism to an audience unfamiliar with Roy's work, and to avoid, as much as possible, abstract academic philosophical language.

This book follows the aim and structure of the talks, breaking it down into three chapters, and where needed further breaking down the chapters into sections. As the editor I made the decision how each chapter would be structured, what footnotes to add, and where I felt it would be helpful to support understanding, I created tables and figures.

Chapter One begins with Basic or Original Critical Realism (BCR). It is possible to see Roy here exploring dualism in the world, or splits, from Ontology vs. Epistemology, Facts vs. Values, Mind vs. Body, Structure vs. Agency. In offering the view of the transitive and intransitive domains, Roy is able to show that we can collapse the dualism, making space for The Real, The Actual, and The Empirical.

Chapter Two Dialectical Critical Realism (DCR), deepens this inquiry by exploring duality or constellation. It points to the importance of absence and negativity. In which we absent ills and constraints by recognising what is absent in our knowledge of the world

Chapter Three The Philosophy of metaReality (PMR), moves into the most controversial area of Roy's work: that of thinking ontology as non-duality. However, if we move slightly away from non-duality as the spiritual experience and think about non-duality from its philosophical view, it is possible to see that at the deep ontological level of alethic truth we share axial rationality (we all act the same) and universal solidarity (we are all the same).

Dedication

This book is dedicated to the memory of Ram Roy Bhaskar (1944–2014)

I would also like to thank my partner Anne. She spent the summer of 2015 working her way through hours of, what at times were, challenging recordings of Roy speaking, creating the transcripts that I worked on to produce this book.

Without you Anne, there would not have been this book. Thank you.

And I have to thank Donald Clark, it was his support, creativity, vision, and the hours he spent listening to me taking about Critical Realism that helped shape this book.

Thank you friend.

...*"For all intents and purposes you could say, well, he is a philosopher, he has written so many books and there are people who are discussing his ideas. But that does not necessarily make me feel whole, it depends what people are doing with the ideas."*

Roy Bhaskar (2010: 21) The Formation of Critical Realism

Chapter One

Dualism

Basic Critical Realism

Live Stream took place 3rd May 2014

"What has been called 'original', 'basic' or 'first wave' critical realism was constructed on a double argument from experimental and applied activity in natural sciences such as physics and chemistry. This double argument was, on the one hand, for the revindication of ontology, or the philosophical study of being, as distinct from and irreducible to epistemology, or the philosophical study of knowledge; and, on the other hand, for a new radically non-Humean ontology allowing for structure, difference and change in the world, as distinct from the flat uniform ontology implicit in the Humean theory of causal laws as constant conjunctions of atomistic events or as invariant empirical regularities – a theory which underpins the doctrines of almost all orthodox philosophy of science."

Roy Bhaskar (2010: 1) Interdisciplinarity and Climate Change: Transforming Knowledge and Practice for Our Global Future

Introduction and The Six Features of Critical Realism

This is the first of three talks, which constitute a kind of introduction to critical realism. To begin with, I am going to say a little bit about the divisions of critical realism, and the divisions within the stages of critical realism. It is customary to talk about three phases of critical realism: the first phase is called *Basic [or Original] Critical Realism*, the second is called *Dialectical Critical Realism* and the third is known as the *Philosophy of metaReality*.

In this first talk, I will be discussing basic or original critical realism, which is pre-supposed by the other two stages of critical realism. Basic critical realism is itself divided, if you like, into three: the first is called *Transcendental Realism*, which is the philosophy of science; the second is called *Critical Naturalism*, which is the philosophy of social science; the third is known as the *Theory of Explanatory Critique,* which is a form of ethics. Before I actually launch into basic critical realism, I want to say something by way of introduction about the critical realist approach to philosophy and the critical realist approach to critical realism, which I am going to divide into six main features.

The first feature is philosophical under-labouring
The second feature is seriousness
The third feature is immanent critique
The fourth feature philosophy as a pre-supposition
The fifth feature is enhanced reflexivity or transformative practice
The sixth feature is the principle of hermeticism

Table One: The Six Features of Critical Realism

Under-labouring

The first - philosophical under-labouring - gives us the point of critical realism that I can best introduce this by reading a quote from John Locke who initiated the metaphor of under-labouring.

"The commonwealth of learning is not at this time without master-builders, whose mighty designs in advancing the sciences, will leave lasting monuments to the admiration of posterity; but every one must not hope to be a Boyle, or a Sydenham; and in an age that produces such masters as the great Huygenius, and the incomparable Mr. Newton, with some others of that strain; it is ambition enough to be employed as an under-labourer in clearing the ground a little, and removing some of the rubbish that lies in the way to knowledge."[1]

So that is the aim of critical realism: to remove the rubbish that prevents us knowing the world. And of course that presupposes that there is some rubbish there but I think most people who have any experience, actually living, are aware that we are surrounded by our systems of thoughts and beliefs which leave much to be desired and effectively act as obstacles to gaining knowledge of the world.

---

1 John Locke (1632–1704), British philosopher. An Essay Concerning Human Understanding, Epist., P. 9, ed. P. Nidditch, Oxford, Clarendon Press (1975).

Seriousness

The second point is seriousness and this concerns the unity of theory and practice. A lot of philosophy is frankly unserious. I will give you an example of what I mean by an unserious philosophical position: this would be the position that the great British empiricist David Hume[2] articulated when he said: *"There's no better reason to leave the building by the ground floor than by the second floor window."*

If you think about it that is absurd, it is unserious because Hume did not actually believe it; if he had believed it then he would have tried to leave buildings by the second floor window on at least 50 per cent of occasions, which of course he did not do. The reason he did not do it was that he knew there was a force - *gravity* - that would have pulled him to the ground. Gravity was a force Hume could not satisfactorily put into his philosophical position and so he was prepared to offer an absurd and contradictory epistemological point of view.[3] Another example from the

---

2 David Hume (7 May 1711 – 25 August 1776)

3 For Bhaskar, something is fundamentally amiss with philosophy. There is something mysterious in the way that the problems it generates – for example, those grouped around Humean scepticism – seem to have nothing to say to a common-sense understanding of the world. Hume himself contrasted the skeptical products of his philosophical reflection with the experience of the world he enjoyed with his backgammon-playing friends. For all that we are said not to be able to prove that a law of gravity exists, we tend to leave the building by the ground-floor exit in preference to the second-floor window. There is something artificial and unserious in the sense that philosophical problems are ultimately unresolvable, rather than possessing 'real, multiple and possibly contradictory geo-historical grounds and conditions' (Bhaskar 2008b:315). There is also something unsatisfactory, and in Bhaskar's term detotalising, in seeing the problems of philosophy as matters

same philosopher, David Hume, of unseriousness is that he said: *"There is no better reason to prefer the destruction of my little finger to that of the whole world."*[4] Now this again is absurd because surely we would all feel that if there was a genuine choice like that we should sacrifice our little finger for the sake of the survival of the whole world. Actually, Hume's statement is worse than that because of course if you choose the whole world then you lose your little finger anyway, so it is really is pointless not to choose your little finger.

What critical realism is concerned with doing is to produce a philosophy which you would walk, *to produce a talk which you can walk*, to produce a philosophy that you can live by and act by in the world. If there is something that I or some other critical realist says today which you find we are not practising then you can rightly indict us out of being unserious. So far, we have seen that critical realism is concerned with removing the rubbish in the way of knowledge, and it is concerned to produce a philosophy that you can act on.

Immanent Critique

The third feature of critical realist philosophy, or the critical realist approach to philosophy, is that of Immanent Critique. Immanent critique means that when we are criticising or assessing a system of thought, we do so from inside. We do not put forward our own objections against the system, we look for something within the system

---

for a distinct discipline sequestered within the walls of the academy, away from worldly activity. Norrie A (2010: 84)

4 (Ed) The actual quote is 'Tis not contrary to reason to prefer the destruction of the whole world to the scratching of my finger."

that we can appeal to and perhaps that we accept which the system itself cannot sustain. A little reflection will show you that only this kind of internal or immanent critique will actually cause a transformation in the beliefs of the people who support or hold the system because it shows there is something wrong from within it, that they are holding incompatible views and that they need to adjust some of it.

Philosophy as a pre-supposition

Then the fourth feature that critical realist philosophy involves is about our conception of our philosophy; in which it talks about the same world that we live in and that we have. There is only one world and this is what philosophy talks about. However, the way in which philosophy talks about the world is to bring into light pre-suppositions of our thought or practice which we are not normally aware of.

You can give an example of this if you think of the concept of the "thing".[5] If you look around your room now and I was to ask you how many things there are in the room, you would be at a bit of a loss because you could obviously count the tables and chairs, or perhaps you

---

5 Bhaskar accepts this ontological understanding of 'thing' as well and elaborates on the internal unity that is a requirement of 'thinghood': 'An entity counts as a "thing" if it possesses sufficient internal complexity, organisation, structure or coherence to count as a unit (or system) or a class (or part) of such units or a complex of relations between or within such units or classes or parts, or if it consists in any earthed function of any of the foregoing' (Bhaskar 2009; 218). Moreover, he argues that, especially in light of recent natural science, the concept of a thing exceeds and so must be distinguished from that of an ordinary material object, for there are things such as powers, fields, gases, genetic codes, and electronic structures. McWherter D (2013: 7)

could count the people but then what about the molecules constituting the tables and chairs.

What about the room as a whole, does that count as a thing in the room? A little reflection will show that this kind of question is ambiguous. Similarly, if I ask you how many events are going on now in our interaction, the notion of an event, it could be uttering a particular sentence or it could be you listening to me, or it could be both, again it is a very ambiguous one.

What critical realist philosophy, and what it regards philosophy at its best is doing, is to bring out what is pre-supposed by our substantive practices. What, one might want to know, such as what does the practice of shopping involve. To choose a more theory of knowledge type example, what does the practice of experimentation have presupposed about the world? If we employ immanent critique and at the same time, what we are trying to do is to analyse our presuppositions of our social practices, we can now look at what a critical realist philosophically accounts of some field such as science or social science could aspire to. We could say that insofar as where critics of the philosophies of natural science say, that they do not give a correct or sufficiently deep, adequate theory or philosophical theory of the practice of natural science.

Enhanced reflexivity / Transformative practice

The fifth feature of critical realism is enhanced reflexivity or transformative practice, this is what critical realism would hope to be able to do is to enhance our reflexivity[6] as scientists so that we have a better theory of what we assume more or less we have been correctly doing. But when you come to the field of social science, it is not at all clear that you could be at all content with what social science is producing because our philosophies of social sciences, and our particular theories and systems within social science, are very contradictory. What we could hope to do is give a better account of our social science and a better account of the world it studies, and that would not so much enhance our reflexivity but transform our practice. So increasingly, as we go on in this series of talks, we will see the transformative or critical function of critical realism moving to the fore.

The principle of Hermeticism

The last feature of a critical realist approach to philosophy that I mentioned is also very important; this I call the principle of Hermeticism, after the legendary Egyptian philosopher known to us by the Greek name Hermes.[7] The principle of Hermeticism states: do not accept anything that I say just because I say it.

---

6 I have stressed that the single most important criterion of philosophy is reflexivity, the absence of theory–practice inconsistency. Thus if Hume claims that he has no better reason for going out of the ground floor door than the second floor window and he always goes out of the ground floor door and never by the second floor window then we know without further ado that his system is fundamentally flawed. Similarly if an academician cannot situate himself within his discourse, cannot situate himself in the story he tells, then we know that he has left something crucial out. Bhaskar (2012b: 309)

7 (Ed) Hermes Trismegistus, a combination of Greek god Hermes and Egyptian god Thoth, is placed in the early days of the oldest dynasties of Egypt. Some authorities regard him as a contemporary

What I say, insofar as is true, you ought to be able to work out and establish for yourself. This is a very important feature of critical realism, it means that if I or some other critical realist figure says something about how we explain an event, you do not just sit back and take notes about it but when you go home or to work and try to explain something that is happening there, the theory that we give of your practice should work. This is all part of being serious, and if it is serious for me then it has got to be serious for you and it has to work in practice.[8]

---

of Abraham, and some Jewish traditions go so far as to claim that Abraham acquired a portion of his mystical knowledge from Hermes himself.

8 (Ed) If you would like to explore the Six Features of Critical Realism further I would recommend reading Bhaskar (2013: 11-12) Prolegomenon, in Engaging with the World: Agency, Institutions, Historical Formation, M. Archer and A. Maccarini (eds) London: Routledge.

Transcendental Realism

I am now going to say a little bit about the beginning of critical realism. By critical realism, I mean the relatively modern philosophy of critical realism,[9] which probably began with the publication of my first book, *A Realist Theory of Science*, in 1975. As I was working on the beginning of critical realism for me, of course was my experience in writing and the experience that the writing reflected of my experience.[10]

At the University of Oxford, I had studied philosophy, politics and economics - a well-known degree, PPE. I liked each of the three subjects roughly equally and so was in a bit of a quandary, because I wanted to pursue my studies at graduate level, as to which to go into, I

---

9 (Ed) Ian Verstegen provides a very good overview on the history of critical realism, which includes American critical realism - http://www.criticalrealism.com/archive/iverstegen_baacr.html (checked 7/10/16)

10 (Ed) For anyone interested in exploring Roy's personal philosophical exploration and the development of critical realism, I would recommend *The Formation of Critical Realism: A Personal Perspective*, Bhaskar, R & Hartwig, M (2010)

came to the conclusion that it would be best to go into Economics.[11] It seemed to me that the most important problems that we faced in the world were economic problems: problems of poverty, problems of gross inequity and so on.

I was particularly concerned, when I was doing my undergraduate economics studies, with the problems of the so-called under-developed countries. Now we call them developing countries and what I was concerned with, what I wanted my post-graduate thesis to be on, was *"The Relevance of Economic Theory for the Problems of Underdeveloped Countries"*, which was my first PhD thesis title. My intuition was that it was not very relevant, that one could not naturally assume that a theory which had been developed to apply to the advanced countries of the West automatically would fit the newly emergent, newly decolonised countries of Asia, Africa and Latin America.

So that was my intuition and I started my graduate studies in a state of great excitement and I will not mention their names but I had very famous tutors who were well versed in both Economics and Philosophy. I quickly concluded that it was an impossible study. Why, because it was clear from the economic methodologies and philosophies of the time that one could not say anything in relation to an economic

---

11 Despite my passion for philosophy, at the end of my finals I eventually opted for economics. This was really because I thought that economics was the most important, or rather the most serious, of the PPE disciplines. While I was very good at solving the puzzles that were posed in philosophy and found the experience very rewarding, they were often in themselves totally trivial, such as is there another mind in the world, does this table exist, or do you have two hands? Bhaskar in Bhaskar, R & Hartwig, M (2010: 23)

theory about the real world. That what you had as an economist were a certain set of axioms and it was your job to develop these axioms to be able to show their implications, and the more unexplained the axioms, the more they did not refer to the world as such (or they were not taken as referring to the world) the stronger the theory. In other words, you could not compare the theory here with the world there. The whole point of my thesis was of course therefore struck down because I could only say it was like there was one hand but not the other hand so, like the sound of one hand clapping my thesis appeared to be a project that was unperceivable.

This itself raised the problem for me: why was economics like that? I went into Philosophy of Science and I read many books on philosophy of science and they talked about things like theory building and modelling and prescribing, explaining, predicting, but there was nothing about the world in these books! They were all about human activities and not about the world. And then I went a bit further and a bit deeper, I was by now quite seriously worried and I went back to Philosophy and I went through Modern Philosophy back to the classical writings of Kant and Hume. There the answer to my quandary, my question, came at me.

They had said *"Thou shalt not do ontology, do not talk about the world."* This was repeated again and again by John Stewart Bell, by Russell, by Wittgenstein.[12] Wittgenstein said: Do not talk about the world, talk about your talk about the world. There it was and so that [the

---

12 John Stewart Bell (June 1928 – October 1990), Bertrand Arthur William Russell, (May 1872 – February 1970), Ludwig Wittgenstein (April 1889 – April 1951)

re-vindication of ontology][13] is what I had to tackle. That led me into the project of a *Realist Theory of Science*,[14] of Transcendental Realism,[15] and therefore of critical realism.

What a Realist Theory of Science had was really two objectives: first, to establish that it was possible to talk about the world, it was possible, legitimate and necessary. Secondly, it argued that we had to have a new understanding, a new account of the world because the old philosophies, the old epistemologies had in fact not been not talking about the world, they had tacitly talked about a very specific kind of world. The kind of world they were implicitly assuming was a world which was defined by the Humean theory of causality, which was the lynch-pin underpinning the deductive-normalogical (D-N)[16] model of explanation and all the theories of orthodox philosophies of science. This

---

13 Obviously I knew I would have to do this, but the theme of the critique of ideologies that masquerade as and stand in the way of knowledge was already very important. I think the transcendental revindication of ontology and the understanding that the scientific process involves a transformation of our beliefs, and gives us access to a world that is not immediately apparent, is vitally important for general emancipation, and that is the enduring message of the book [A Realist Theory of Science] Bhaskar in Bhaskar, R & Hartwig, M (2010: 55).

14 Bhaskar (1975/2008a). A Realist Theory of Science. London and New York: Routledge

15 The important thing I think is that, first, transcendental realism does not underwrite any particular science or any particular practice of science; it is quite consistent with a critique of scientific practices in a particular domain. Rather, what it does is ask what must the world be like for the scientific practice – experimental activity – that our tradition takes as paradigmatic to be possible, intelligible, successful and ongoing. Bhaskar in Bhaskar, R & Hartwig, M (2010: 58)

16 [...] the 'deductive-nomological' or 'D-N' model of explanation, [...] developed by Carl Gustav Hempel (1905–97), holds that a claim has been explained when it can be deduced from general scientific laws or law-like statements called 'covering laws. Baggini J & Fosl P (2010: 47)

theory of causal laws said that in order to invoke a causal law is to talk about a constant conjunction of atomistic events. That presupposes implicitly that the world is fixed, repetitive, unstructured and undifferentiated. That the world here is the same as the world in South Africa, and in Siberia, and in Burma and that the world today is the same as it was in 1750 and as it will be in 2050.

Of course, we know that is rubbish, or at least I hope that is rubbish, but that is what was pre-supposed by the Humean theory of causal laws and the doctrine that was science is about establishing empirical regularities, constant conjunctions of events.

A Realist Theory of Science was structured around two arguments: an argument for ontology and an argument for a new ontology, most of the important distinctions of basic or original philosophy of critical realism stem from this dual argument and those two arguments encapsulated in it. The argument for ontology is the argument against its reduction to epistemology in modern philosophy. Now for those of you who are not familiar with these terms, epistemology is the theory of knowledge.

Ontology, I should have said this before, is the theory of being, it is the study of being. Critical realism argues that to understand science you need to constitute two dimensions: an ontological, or I called an intransitive dimension of a world which is studied by science and its epistemological or a transitive dimension of a world which is a social world in which science is articulated and developed which studies the intransitive objects of science.[17]

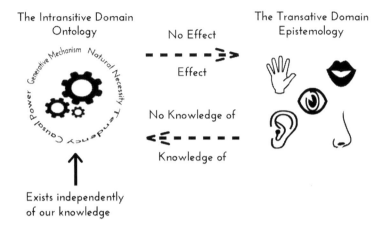

The Intransitive Domain
Ontology

No Effect

The Transative Domain
Epistemology

Effect

No Knowledge of

Knowledge of

Exists independently
of our knowledge

Figure One: The Intransitive & Transitive

We need both of these and I argued that not having a sufficiently strong concept of both was the source of many problems in existing theories of knowledge.

This argument for ontology was the argument against the epistemic fallacy,[18] the reductionist ontology to epistemology or for an

---

17 If men ceased to exist sound would continue to travel and heavy bodies fall to the earth in exactly the same way, though ex hypothesi there would be no-one to know it. Let us call these, in an unavoidable technical neologism, the intransitive objects of knowledge. The transitive objects of knowledge are Aristotelian material causes. They are the raw materials of science—the artificial objects fashioned into items of knowledge by the science of the day. They include the antecedently established facts and theories, paradigms and models, methods and techniques of inquiry available to a particular scientific school or worker. Bhaskar (2008a: 11)

18 (...) the 'epistemic fallacy'. This consists in the view that statements about being can be reduced to or analysed in terms of statements about knowledge; i.e. that ontological questions can always

intransitive as well as a transitive dimension and for what critical realists call the holy[19] trinity[20].

The holy trinity of critical realism or basic critical realism is the compatibility of three things: *Ontological Realism*, that is realism about the world, *Epistemological Relativity*, that is the idea that the beliefs are socially produced, fallible, unchangeable and changing so our knowledge is relative. And the third principle is that of *Judgemental Rationality* and this says that even though our knowledge is relative, we can produce in particular contexts, strong arguments for preferring one set of beliefs, one set of theories about the world to another.

So, scientists have strong arguments for believing that the Einsteinian system is superior to, more true if you like, than the Newtonian system although the Newtonian system is splendidly applicable in practically all contexts of its use. So on this axis of the

---

be transposed into epistemological terms. The idea that being can always be analysed in terms of our knowledge of being, that it is sufficient for philosophy to 'treat only of the network, and not what the network describes. Bhaskar (2008a: 26)

19 (Ed) Holy is a play on the word Holes, as in representing absence or 2E. We will cover 2E and absence in the next chapter when we explore dialectical critical realism.

20 1) ontological realism: the dimension of intransitive objects of knowledge, which exist and also act in an independent manner from our theories about them, the transitive space. Critical realism accepts (2) epistemic relativity: the idea that beliefs are products of society, which implies that all knowledge is a historically transient entity; in other words, our criteria for truth and values are not externally situated from our particular historical time as we see that our knowledge changes through time. Epistemic relativity also includes fallibilism, the idea that our beliefs may turn out to be false. In addition, critical realism opens a space for the possibility of (3) judgemental rationality: the idea that individuals can make decisions between relative beliefs, which itself assumes both epistemic relativity and historicity." Nunez, I (2014: 55)

argument, the argument for ontology, the central theorem here is the compatibility of ontological realism, epistemological relativism and judgemental rationality.

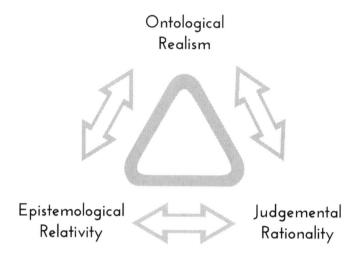

Ontological Realism

Epistemological Relativity

Judgemental Rationality

Figure Two: The Holy Trinity of Critical Realism

Now, when it comes to the argument for a new ontology, there are two crucial distinctions here: there is the distinction between open and closed systems and the old philosophy of science, empiricism and neo-Kantianism most philosophical systems generally presuppose the closed system. Whereas I argued the world was an open system, only in closed systems, and especially in the experimentally closed systems, do you actually get conjunctions of events. In the open system world in which we live and act there are no constant conjunctions and that is the first ontological distinction. Then the second is the distinction between structures, generative mechanisms[21] and events, or as I put it between the

---

21 Now once it is granted that mechanisms and structures may be said to be real, we can provide an interpretation of the independence of causal laws from the patterns of events, and a fortiori of

domain of the real, the actual and the empirical. The empirical is the baseline of our empiricist and neo-Kantian[22] philosophy but for critical realism there are events, which have not been experienced, you have to have the distinction between the actual and the empirical and then when you get to the actual, there is not only the events but the structures and mechanisms that produce or generate them. These structures and mechanisms that generate events are the true objects of scientific understanding, and they apply in open and closed systems alike. In other words, they apply where you do not get constant conjunctions of events.

There are still real mechanisms at work and that is a presupposition I argued of experimental unapplied activity, without it, we would not be able to apply our knowledge of physics, chemistry or any science, including possibly the social sciences at all. This is a crucial distinction between structures and mechanisms, the domain of the real on the one hand and the events, which they generate, which are also real but which are actual as well.

---

the rationale of experimental activity. For the real basis of this independence lies in the independence of the generative mechanisms of nature from the events they generate. Such mechanisms endure even when not acting; and act in their normal way even when the consequents of the law-like statements they ground are, owing to the operation of intervening mechanisms or countervailing causes, unrealized. It is the role of the experimental scientist to exclude such interventions, which are usual; and to trigger the mechanism so that it is active. The activity of the mechanism may then be studied without interference. And it is this characteristic pattern of activity or mode of operation that is described in the statement of a causal law. It is only under closed conditions that there will be a one-to-one relationship between the causal law and the sequence of events. Bhaskar (2008a: 36)

22 Immanuel Kant (April 1724 – February 1804)

	Domain of the Real	Domain of the Actual	Domain of the Empirical
Mechanisms	✓		
Events	✓	✓	
Experiences	✓	✓	✓

Figure Three: Domains

So now just as there was a central fallacy which underpinned the empiricist and Kantian mainstream position at the level of the argument for ontology, which are called the epistemic fallacy, so there is a central error here and this is the error of Actualism.[23] This is the error of our reducing the possible and the reality of powers and tendencies and liabilities to actuality. Probably the most important feature of this new philosophy of science, which I called transcendental realism, was the idea that reality was stratified and there are three important senses to the concept of stratification in transcendental realism. There is the distinction between structures or mechanisms on the one hand and events and their conjunctions on the other, or between the domains of the real and the actual.

Then there is a sense in which this stratification is multi-tiered in reality. Thus the tables and chairs in this room I am speaking from are constituted by molecules with in turn are constituted by atoms which are constituted by electrons which are constituted by quantum mechanical

---

23 See Actualism entry in Hartwig M (2007) The Dictionary of Critical Realism and http://plato.stanford.edu/entries/actualism/

fields or singularities or quarks. In other words, you have tiers of strata in science that it progressively reveals. Then there is a third centre of stratification, which involves emergence.

An emergence is a very important feature of transcendental realism and critical realism. The best way to think about emergence is in terms of concrete examples. We can take the example of body and mind and for critical realists mind is an emergent power, what I characterise as symphonic emergent power[24] of matter, or of body, if you like. These three features are crucial here. First, the way in which the emergent power or property is unilaterally existentially dependent on the more basic power, property, or feature. Mind is unilaterally existentially dependent on body. That means you do not have, as far as you know, mind without bodies.

The second feature is that mind is taxonomically irreducible to body. That is to say, when you have mind you have features such as motives, intentionality, reason, plan, purpose, which cannot be reduced or unpacked in terms of the properties of bodies. The third feature is equally important – in fact, it is the most dramatic when you think about it – and that is mind is causally irreducible to and efficacious in the realm of body. That is to say, once you have minds, bodies are different.

Once you have minds, they intervene at the level of bodies, which is the way we have been intervening at the level of climate, and of course, this is what is involved in industry. This is what is involved in action; we produce changes in the material world, if you think about it

---

24 See note 48 further

this is what is involved in any human action at all. If I ask Rebecca,[25] who is sitting here beside me, I am feeling a bit cold, and ask her if she could go and get a jersey from my office a few floors up. She will move the lift, go up to my office, and move things around in my office, and she is of course moving the whole time and she will bring back my jersey. All of them will be a material changes at the level of body. Therefore, these are three important features of an emergent power: three important features of an emergent level or emergent property in being.

1. *Mind is unilaterally existentially dependent on body*
2. *Mind is taxonomically irreducible to body*
3. *Mind is causally irreducible to and efficacious in the realm of body*

I want to dwell for a bit on this feature of this new philosophy of science, which is what makes it so exciting. That is when we are doing science what we are concerned with is not really to produce a repetition or a confirmation or even a falsification of our experience; what we are primarily concerned to do is to understand the causes of our experience or the causes of the events that we perceive in the world. What science is doing is something exciting and new. It is moving from a level of reality that we do understand, like, say, the levels of tables and chairs, to the level

---

25 (Ed) Rebecca, was not only Roy's support and partner, she was instrumental in dealing with the complexity of room bookings, Roy's diary, and his wellbeing during the three months Donald and I worked with Roy.

of what explains them, which at any moment of time we do not understand. So science is a wondrous thing and it is telling us about what is recondite, what lies behind what we do know and what explains what we can observe or see. It is telling us something new. When Newton introduced the idea of gravity, he was telling us something new, science is exciting and is continually expanding the frontiers of what we know.

Let us go back to our popular understanding of the philosophy of science. The empiricism that we had, the empiricism of neo-Kantianism that we had, had come unstuck on what is known as the problem of induction.[26] The problem of how you move from a certain number of observations of a conjunction (or two things going together) to the assumption that they always go together.

How do you move from all the swans in your experience being white, or that of your community being white, to a universal statement like "all swans are white"? Well, of course, Europeans, when they got to Latin America, to South America and to Australia, quickly discovered that it was not the case that all swans were white, many swans were black as well. The possibility of discovering a black swan threatens even our knowledge when we do not have a disconfirming, falsifying example like that.

---

26 The traditional problem of induction is the problem of what warrant we have for reasoning from particular instances to general statements (induction proper) or from observed to unobserved or past to future instances (eduction). Bhaskar (2008a: 207)

So if you take the statement: all emeralds are green, one of our recent philosophers of science, Nelson Goodman,[27] pointed out that this statement could be true up to midnight tonight, and after midnight tonight all emeralds could suddenly become blue.[28] All the evidence we have for all emeralds are green is equally evidence for the statement that all emeralds are *grue*, when *grue* means green up to midnight tonight and blue thereafter. In fact, there is no resolution to the problem of induction within the existing actualist problem field within a problem field that reduces knowledge and the world to one level.

What a critical realist scientist, or what a critical realist philosopher, would do is to follow what a real scientist does, and after a real scientist arrives at what looks like a meaningful regularity in, say, the laboratory, the scientist tries to fathom out why it is that these two predicates - being green and being an emerald - are conjoined. What is it about emeralds that make them green? That is what the scientist asks and the scientist goes on to investigate the nature, the intrinsic qualities of emeralds, in virtue of which they do manifest the property of being green. In other words, the real scientist follows critical realism in moving

---

27 (Ed) For a detailed discussion on Goodman, Induction and Grue see Chapter 2, If this were an emerald it would be grue: problems and riddles of induction: Cohnitz D & Rossberg M, (2006)

28 Now either 'all emeralds are green' is law-like or it is not. If it is not the Goodmanesque alternative 'all emeralds are grue' is equally admissible. For it is then ex hypothesi purely accidental that all emeralds happen to be green. On the other hand, to suppose that 'all emeralds are green' is law-like is to suppose that there is a reason, located in its crystalline structure of chemical composition, why it differentially reflects light the way it does. Now given that structure, emeralds must, to normal observers under standard conditions, look green. So anything which looked blue could not possess that structure, and hence would not be an emerald at all. Bhaskar (2008a: 214)

towards the identification of a structure or a mechanism, which will explain the actual regularity that is observed. Now, it is possible to make out a good rationale in the development of science in which science proceeds from knowledge of one level of reality to knowledge of the level of reality, which explains that original level.

It goes like this: I use the acronyms **D R E I (C).**[29]

D is **Description**, and that is the first thing that one does in science; that is describes the phenomena as accurately as one can. The second is R and this is **Retroduction**[30] is very important it is neither induction nor deduction as distinct from both; it is the most characteristically scientific logical move. In the retroductive moment, a scientist imagines a mechanism or structure, which, if it were true, would explain the event or regularity in question. It is a use of the imagination to posit explanatory mechanisms and structures.

Now clearly you can posit any number of explanatory mechanisms or structures. So the third step in the dialectic of scientific development and discovery is given by the E, that is you **Eliminate** those which are false.

---

29 (Ed) DREI(C) is applied explanation of events within a closed system such as within a laboratory. If one were working within an open system such as a social system, climate change, psychoanalysis, or disability studies then a critical realist would use the RRREI(C) model. For a complete explanation of RRREI(C) see Bhaskar (2011: 3-6)

30 (Ed) For the difference between retroduction and retrodiction see Steve Fleetwood, S & Hesketh A (2010: 243-245)

Then at a fourth level you come to the very exciting thing in which you can *Identify* a real mechanism or structure at work. The fifth step is (C), *[Correct]* which, when able, allows you to correct the results you are obtained so far - so you get DREI(C).

D is Description

R is Retroduction

E is Elimination

I is Identification

C is Correction

Table Two: DREIC

Note two things: 1) When you get to the I, then you have a reason independent of manifest behaviour or observable properties, why a thing must do or must be the way it is. According to the problem of induction there is no reason to expect that the next drink of water that I have will quench my thirst in the way that the last did; or there is no reason to expect why, if I went outside and took a walk, that I would get wet if it was raining, any more than I did last time.

But now we have a knowledge of the properties and powers intrinsic to things which explains why they behave the way they do, that is the first thing to note: that you have a genuine explanation independent of the phenomena which explains it.

2) Secondly, when you get to this level, when you have identified the generative mechanism or structure at work that is not the end of science, the next thing you do is, of course, ask the question: why does that happen? Why is the world that way? And that moves you on to a new cycle of scientific discovery and development, and so you have a repeated DREI(C).

This is the essence of the transcendental realists' philosophy of science, if I can put it like that: a view of science as a social process concerned to study a world outside it which is moving from one level of reality we have knowledge of to a deeper level which explains it in an indefinite process.

Critical Naturalism

We have looked at the philosophy of science in general: *Transcendental Realism*. Now I want to turn more specifically to the philosophy of social science: *Critical Naturalism*. When you look at social science, you cannot make some of the assumptions that you can make in the case of the natural sciences, for example, about the independence of the intransitive world from the transitive world.

It is best to look at it separately; in fact, the principle of immanent critique means that we cannot just naively apply our findings from the philosophy of natural science to the philosophy of social science because we must do an independent study as to what extent the two realms are in fact straightforwardly comparable.

We start again, afresh, in the philosophy of the social sciences and here we have to use again the principle of immanent critique. I should mention that the reason why I focused on experimental activity in my arguments in relation to natural science was because this was the premise that everyone agreed on (empiricists, neo-Kantians, etc.) all believed this was a very important feature and it was not me importing my own standpoint into the philosophy of natural science.

So in relation to the philosophy of social science and social theory generally, there was a feature which was almost undeniable and that was that everywhere, wherever you looked, there were dualisms. What were these dualisms? There was a dualism between structure and agency, there was a dualism between society and individuals, there was a dualism between conceptuality or language, and behaviour or materiality. Then there was a dualism between mind and body, the dualism between reason and cause, the dualism between fact and value, and even the dualism between theory and practice. The role of critical naturalism was to try to resolve these dualisms by giving a fairer account of the subject in question.

Let me go through a few of these resolutions. Let us take the old conundrum of structure and agency; what I said in my second book, *The Possibility of Naturalism*[31], was that structure and agency had been wrongly conceived; that a structure was always necessary for agency, and at the same time agency reproduced or transformed structure.

So the sense in which structure is always necessary is a sense in which it always pre-exists any round of human agency, because you cannot engage in a speech act unless you have a pre-existing structure of language: you cannot get married unless there is a pre-existing structure of marriage, or family structure. If you think about it deeply enough you

---

31 Bhaskar [1979] 2014. The Possibility of Naturalism: A Philosophical Critique of the Contemporary Human Sciences. London: Routledge.

will find that this is so whatever act you are thinking of, it always pre-supposes the prior existence of structure. Therefore, structure always comes first when we are talking about agency and structure.

Equally crucial is the fact that structure would not be on going. Structure although always pre-existent would not be on going without agency. If no one got married, if no one spoke, than the structures of marriage or family and of language would not survive, they would fade out, language would not be a living one, and the practice of marriage or whatever would belong to the past. The role of structure and agency that I defined in the *Transformational Model of Social Activity*[32] involved the pre-existence of structure and the necessary continuity of structure through being reproduced or transformed in agency.

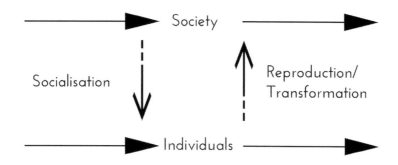

Figure Four: The Transformational Model of Social Activity[33]

---

32 The TMSA, upon which social structure is a necessary condition for, and medium of, intentional agency, which is in turn a necessary condition for the reproduction or transformation of social forms. Bhaskar (2008b: 154)

33 (Ed) For a detailed overview of TMSA see Collier A (1994: 141-151). An Introduction to Roy Bhaskar's Critical Realism London: Verso

At the time, I wrote my second book; Anthony Giddens[34] formulated his well-known theory of structuration. They were both published, as it happens, in 1979. Tony Giddens invited me to lunch, a very nice restaurant in Greek Street, I think, in Soho in London. We both agreed that our models were very similar and mutually supportive. Then, over the years, a friend and colleague of mine, Margaret Archer[35], pointed out that this was not so. She said, correctly, that my model was very different from Tony Giddens's because of the central role time plays in it. For Tony Giddens it is as if when you go to bed at night the structures pack up. You know, you can imagine dons in a Cambridge college going to bed and then in the morning, they kind of re-invent the rules of the college.

This may fit a college in Cambridge but it does not fit most of social life. The most obvious fact of social life is the presence of the past and this imposes an enormous constraint. If you look around the room you are sitting in you will see that the room is in a house, which was built at a certain time, and the furniture belongs to a certain age and we are here talking about a problem of sociology, a problem that comes from the

---

34 His advice has been sought by political leaders from Asia, Latin America and Australia, as well as from the US and Europe. He has had a major impact upon the evolution of New Labour in the UK. He took part in the original Blair-Clinton dialogues from 1997 onwards. Retrieved May 20/05/15 http://www.lse.ac.uk/sociology/whoswho/academic/Giddens.aspx

35 Margaret Archer was elected as the first woman President of the International Sociological Association at the 12th World Congress of Sociology. She is a founder member of both the Pontifical Academy of Social Sciences and the Academy of Learned Societies in the Social Sciences and is a trustee of the Centre for Critical Realism. Retrieved May 20/05/15 http://cdh.epfl.ch/page-55771-en.html

nineteenth century, of structure and agency. We are living in a world, which largely we have not created, and that means it is very difficult, unfortunately, for us radicals to transform the world in the way we want to.

Of course, it does not mean that the world cannot be transformed but it just imposes a serious constraint on it. Tony Giddens's model was too voluntaristic,[36] if you like, and Margaret Archer's own model, which she calls a morphogenetic model,[37] is a variant of the transformational model of social activity.

As the years from 1979 went by, I thought one could add something more to the transformational model of social activity in the conception I now call *four-planer social being*. The idea of four-planer social being[38] says that every event in the social world occurs simultaneously on four planes: the plane of material transactions with nature; the plane of

---

36 (Ed) Voluntarism is the theory that the will rather than the intellect is the ultimate principle of reality.

37 See Archer M, Chapter 14, Realism and morphogenesis, in Archer M, Collier A, Bhaskar R, Lawson T, Norrie A, (1998: 356) Critical Realism: Essential Readings: Routledge

38 The transformational model of social activity may be further developed to generate the notion of four-planar social being. This specifies that every social event occurs in at least four dimensions, that of material transactions with nature; that of social interactions between humans; that of social structure proper; and that of the stratification of the embodied personality. These four planes constitute, of course, a necessarily laminated system of their own in so far as reference to any one level or dimension will also necessarily involve reference to the others. In a similar way each social level involved in any applied explanation can not only be situated in the context of four-planar social being, but also in that of a hierarchy of scale, that is of more macroscopic or overlying and less macroscopic or underlying mechanisms. Bhaskar, in Bhaskar et al (2010: 9)

social interactions between people; the plane of social structure sui generis (the economy, society, language, etc.), and then, fourthly, the plane of the stratification of the embodied personality. That is an important development coming out of the transformational model of social activity.

When we turn to the problem of society and the individual, what was very fashionable at the time I wrote The Possibility of Naturalism was a doctrine known as methodological individualism, which asserted that the only real things in the social world were people. The other seeming things that we referred to in social life, such as constitutions, armies, etc., could all be reduced ultimately to individuals and their properties. There was a tendency in social theory and philosophy of social science, which was opposed to this, and they called themselves methodological holists or collectivists.

However, their paradigm of what was an individual was things like crowds and mass behaviour and this was very unfortunate, I think, because if you take an interest in social structure, like a family or economy or a political constitution, they are not at all like mass behaviour, which seems to me to be a socio-psychological phenomena. I argued that what both the holists and the individualists had got wrong was they had failed to understand that society was not about individuals as such, nor was it about something opposed to individuals, rather what the social scientists were about were the persistent relations between individuals. That if you take my paradigm of a family as a sociological topic, what the family is concerned with is a relation between the parents, between the parents and the children, and such like, this gives the social scientist a distinct relational function. Therefore, I think this relationism, as it could be called, is a distinct advance on existing paradigms of that of the individual and the non-individual.

However, in a subsequent reflection I qualified this a little bit, because it gave the impression that the only legitimate object of social science were persisting relations. I do not think this is correct; in fact, I now think you can study social phenomena and social phenomena are constituted at all of seven levels, at least. Taking this in terms of the smallest level first[39], there is this sub-individual level, which one thinks of the unconscious and motives. Then there is the individual level, the level at which a social theorist such as Sartre, or novelist, typically conceive the social world. Then there is the micro social world studied by ethno-methodologists, by Garfinkel's[40] by the Goffman's[41] of the world. Then there is the meso world of classical sociology, which studies the relation between functional types and roles, relations between capitalists and workers or between management and workers, or management and shareholders, or owner-managers and shareholders, or between MPs and citizens. Then there is the macro social which might study, for example, the Norwegian economy as a whole, or Norway as a whole. Then there is the mega level in which your unit of study is whole swathes of space-time, in which you are concerned with things like the development of Islam, or of feudalism. Then there is the planetary level in which you are concerned with the world, the planet or even outside the planet - solar system, could be, as a whole.

---

39 (Ed) The seven levels are further expounded on in Bhaskar's foreword to Edwards P K, & O'Mahoney J, & Vincent S (2014). (See page x Anti-reductionism and Laminated Systems)

40 Harold Garfinkel (October 1917 – April 2011)

41 Erving Goffman (June 1922 – November 1982)

Now taking the third of the dualisms, this was the dualism, which was perhaps the sharpest in the Sixties, Seventies, Eighties - it was the dualism, which was expressed as an opposition between hermeneutics[42] and positivism[43]. So, hermeneuticists argued that the social world was essentially linguistic. If there were extreme, as most of them were, then that was all that was to the social world: language; by 'extreme' I mean Winch[44], Gadamer.[45] If they were non-extreme then they often combined this, as Weber[46] and Habermas[47] did, with some elements of positivism. Where does critical realism stand on this?

Critical realism stands firmly with those who argued that hermeneutics is essential. Social reality is conceptualised reality, but at the same time that does not exhaust social reality because, social reality is also material. To understand the social world we have to understand conceptual and material reality. When you are thinking about homelessness, then, of course, you are thinking about the application of certain concepts and how human species has a concept of a home. However, you are also thinking about the way in which people who are homeless do not have a roof over their heads and get wet and cold at night. It is important to bear these two features of social reality in mind. Social reality is conceptualised, is dependent on our conceptualisation, but

---

42 See Hermeneutics entry in Hartwig M (2007) The Dictionary of Critical Realism and http://plato.stanford.edu/entries/hermeneutics/

43 See Positivism entry in Hartwig M (2007) The Dictionary of Critical Realism

44 Peter Guy Winch (January 1926 – April 1997)

45 Hans-Georg Gadamer (February 1 1900 – March 2002)

46 Karl Emil Maximilian "Max" Weber (April 1864 – June 1920)

47 Jürgen Habermas (born June 1929)

is not exhausted by it and because of that conceptualisations and the language we use, can be criticised subject to critique.

The mind body dualism, we put forward a position, which I called the *Synchronic Emergent Powers Materialism:*[48] that is to say, we saw mind as an emergent power of body. In the case of the dualism between reasons and causes, we saw reasons as causes, as causually efficacious and I put forward a theory of intentional causality.[49]

I would like to offer a brief word about the fact/value dualism. What critical realism sustained here was the idea of facts actually secreting values. The idea of being able to ground our evaluative positions in a scientific or a factual account of the world. What was essential to me here was the criticality of discourse because what happens when you are undergoing an education or when you are having a discussion, whether it is an argument or just an exchange of opinions with someone, is you are uttering a discourse but this discourse is implicitly or explicitly critical. When you learn the theory that the earth goes around the sun, rather than the other way round, when you begin to learn the heliocentric theory, then this is implicitly critical of all the earth-centred views. When you see the earth as curved, then this is implicitly critical of the idea that

---

48 (...) synchronic emergent powers materialism (S.E.P.M.) I have advocated is in support of a conception of mind as a biologically emergent ensemble of powers of matter with irreducible explanatory principles of its own. S.E.P.M. is counterposed to reductionist physicalism (e.g. central state materialism) and behaviourism, which collapse those powers to their physical basis and exercise respectively, and to immaterialist dualism (or idealism) which hypostatise (or transcendentise) them. Bhaskar (2009: 91)

49 Intentional causality [...] the idea that people as biopsychosocial stratified individuals are capable of giving reasons for causes. Nunez I (2014: 27)

you can go in a straight line from one position 400 miles east and carry on walking until you eventually return to where you started. The important point here is to understand that in learning new beliefs and theories about the world we are explicitly or implicitly discarding, changing, getting rid of our old beliefs and theories about the world. It is not just our beliefs about the world that we are getting rid of; we are also implicitly critical of the actions informed by those beliefs.

When you have a new theory about what causes a particular problem and you come to see that witchcraft, you come to revise your ideas of witchcraft. You see that there are not any witches and that therefore burning people as witches is wrong, then you will implicitly change and be critical of your actions and be logically bound to stop behaving in the way you did. You move from having a conatus to change beliefs, to having a conatus to change actions and then in the third step you move to exploring what it is that causes beliefs and actions. If you can say what it is about social structure or perhaps a psychic structure which produces a certain belief which is false, then ceteris paribus you have a negative valuation of that belief or that system or structure, be it social or psychic or whatever.

That is the basis of the theory of *Explanatory Critique*,[50] which I developed, in my third book, *Scientific Realism and Human Emancipation*.[51]

---

50 ...an explanatory critique or metacritique. This involves a substantive explanation of not only what is wrong or inadequate in a system of thought, but why it was believed, that is (considering different modalities of this explanatory form), how it came to be generated, accepted and reproduced. Such a form of critique will of course inevitably pass over to a critique of the objects

Applied Critical Realism

If critical realism is to satisfy the criterion of seriousness, it must be applicable. Furthermore, it is in its applications that, on its own self-understanding, the whole point and value of critical realism as an underlabourer for and occasional midwife of good science lies. So much so that one could say that applied or practical critical realism - critical realism in action, so to speak - is, or should be the soul or heartbeat of critical realist." Roy Bhaskar (2016: 78)

Now, what I want to do for the last half hour or so is to talk a little bit about *Applied Critical Realism*.[52] This is critical realism for use in the open systems of daily life and practice. The first point to note here is

---

generating the inadequate, misleading, or superficial consciousness. It may be further extended to show the full range of the baneful effects of the faulty system of belief, and its causes. Bhaskar (2010: 22)

51 Bhaskar (2009). Scientific Realism and Human Emancipation. London: Routledge

52 (Ed) For a list of books exploring Applied Critical Realism see The Routledge Critical Realism series, Ontological Explorations, New Studies in Critical Realism, Education, Critical Realism: Interventions, and the Journal of Critical Realism

that applied critical realism, any applied critical realist project, is always doubly specific. That is to say, it is specific to the object you are trying to study, the ontology involved. It is specific to where you are in your transitive dimension in terms of knowledge of that project. So there is no general method, there is only a specific method for specific objects given certain epistemological circumstances. The theorem of dual specificity, or applied critical realist research, is a paramount one.

My interest in this particular topic, my interest in terms of time taken thinking and working on it, stemmed from my stay at the Institute of Disability Research in Örebro, Sweden, where I was a guest. My host, Berth Danermark,[53] and critical realist colleague thought it would be a good idea to do some work on the very important topic of interdisciplinarity. When we turn to this topic of Interdisciplinarity,[54] and we were looking particularly at interdisciplinarity in disability studies,[55] we found the sort of reprise of what I had found when I started on my path to critical realism.

There was a lot written about the epistemology, and a lot of it quite socialogically intense and dense of interdisciplinarity. Nevertheless, there was nothing about the ontology, nothing about whether there was something about the nature of the world, which made interdisciplinarity necessary and useful. Of course, there is, but this failure to ask the

---

53 Berth Danermark (born July 1951) is currently a professor at Örebro University in Sweden

54 See Mervyn H. (Ed) (2007) The Dictionary of Critical Realism entry on Interdisciplinarity

55 Bhaskar R & Danermark B (2006) Metatheory, Interdisciplinarity and Disability Research: A Critical Realist Perspective, Scandinavian Journal of Disability Research, 8:4, 278-297, http://dx.doi.org/10.1080/15017410600914329

ontological question had resulted in a great mountain of literature with very little real substance or penetration to it.

If you start from a critical realist standpoint then it will be immediately obvious that because you are dealing with phenomena that are produced in an open system, you are going to have to refer to one or more generative mechanisms or structures. By definition, as only in the closed system that you will have one structure or mechanism, in an open system you always are dealing with what is produced by a multiplicity of mechanisms and structures, so you are always dealing with complexity.

Then again, in open systems you are mainly dealing with mechanisms which operate at different ontological levels of reality: some of them are human, some of them are biological, some of them are organic, some of them inorganic. Then, many of the human ones are social and so you are dealing with various levels of emergence. Complexity and emergence of levels, and indeed of outcomes, are essential constitutive features of the ontology for interdisciplinary work.

When Berth and I started looking at interdisciplinarity in relation to disability studies, we found that disability studies had historically moved through three distinct stages. Thus, in the sixties there was a dominance of the clinical paradigm, the medical model, in which, basically, disabilities were regarded as... well, let me put it like this, in which, basically, to have a disability was to have a physical and biological problem and that was the end of it. There would be various ways of clinically treating or dealing with this problem. Naturally, there was a reaction to this biological or clinical reductionism and it came in the form of the so-called social model, which was really an economic model because in the later sixties and seventies the argument was that there would not be problem of disabilities if the distribution of resources was right. If every room was accessible, there would not be a problem for people who could not walk with their legs and, similarly, with respect to other disabilities. Obviously, the economic model had a good point against the clinical model, but you could ask was there a point in the clinical model as well, which had been retained?

By the eighties, a third model or paradigm arose which was the cultural model. This was the social constructionist paradigm in which it was argued that, really, there would not be a problem about disabilities if we all used the correct language and if we had the correct attitudes to it. So, the whole question of disability turned on another form of reductionism. We had these three forms of reductionism, all of them touching a level of truth but all of them being woefully reductionist.

In order to create an anti-reductionist paradigm, Berth and I took the concept of a *Laminated System*, a concept that had been used by a critical realist friend of ours before us, Andrew Collier.[56] A laminated system, we said, was the system, which was composed of a multiplicity of different levels, reference to each of which was necessary in order to understand, or give and adequate account of, the phenomena in question.

There are different types of laminated systems that we formulated, the model of four-planar social being, which I have already referred to, the seven-tier model of a social being, the seven levels of scale, those are

---

56 A. Collier, 'Dialectic in Marxism and critical realism', in A. Brown, S. Fleetwood and J. M. Roberts (eds) Critical Realism and Marxism, London: Routledge, 2002, pp. 155–67.

forms of laminated system, as well as the particular model we introduced in which we argued that reference to physical to biological to psychological to socio-economic and to socio-cultural and normative features were all necessary in a typical case of a disability, that they were all necessary for it. There are others, models of laminated system including one involving overlapping spacio temporalities that there is no time to go into here.[57]

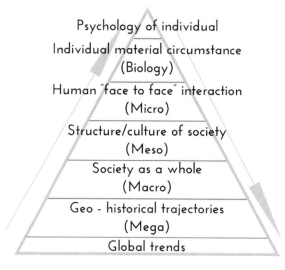

Figure Five: Laminated System

Epistemologically, we argued that what was important in any interdisciplinary context was a form of transdisciplinarity in which we could creatively exploit cognitive resources from different fields, as creative natural scientists do when they are model building. Two other

57 (Ed) For an excellent application of a laminated system, see Leigh Price. "Critical Realist versus Mainstream Interdisciplinarity. Journal of Critical Realism 2014; 13(1), 52-76. Which can be download at: http://goo.gl/pzl4hf as of October 2016, and see Bhaskar's Introduction to Edwards P K, & O'Mahoney J, & Vincent S (2014)

things I said were absolutely essential: the first of this was cross-disciplinary understanding, that is the capacity of me as a sociologist to understand what you as a geographer or a geologist are saying, and vice versa. This cross-disciplinary understanding is something which is very difficult to achieve in practice but it is absolutely essential for interdisciplinary work.

Then the final step is effective epistemic integration and these two moves, at an epistemological level in interdisciplinarity, these two moves can be underpinned by two principles from the *Philosophy of metaReality* that I will be going into in our third session, principles called universal solidarity and axial rationality. Universal solidarity[58] says it is always, in principle, possible to understand anyone else and axial rationality says that where you have a conflict or dispute between parties, it is always possible to arrive at an optimal resolution of it. Those principles give a bit of hope for good interdisciplinary work.

However, there are huge obstacles to it at the moment and these obstacles pose serious problems to coming up with effective solutions in relation to climate change, for instance, where one has typically the great difficulty that people trained in the arts and humanities and the social sciences find in understanding the natural sciences and vice versa. Even more of a problem is the existence of economics as a science, which appears to be closed to other sciences, other social sciences, and this is something that can only be transformed by the immanent development of such a science.

---

58 See further in text - Conflict Resolution and Peace (p 162)

One could compare this with the difficulties of working in an interdisciplinary team when there are surgeons and consultant surgeons and social workers in the same team, because the existing status hierarchies are so tilted in favour of the consultant surgeon that they will not typically pay sufficient account of the views of social workers and nurses and physiotherapists and of course the patient themselves and their families, all of whom are equally necessary to the healing of the problem.[59]

Generally, the pathos of the interdisciplinary predicament can be seen by the fact that in interdisciplinary work we are dealing with an integrated problem with dis-integrated sciences and disciplines. We need a comparable level of integration in our thought and action to achieve effective responses to many of the applied problems we face in the world today.

There are a number of conditions for successful and for a transformation in the prospects for interdisciplinary work: the first condition is to clearly disambiguate ontological and epistemological questions, because typically in the interdisciplinary context the same thing will be being referred to in different ways by members of different disciplines or language communities or professions.

Secondly, a second principle, is anti-reductionism, and the third is using a laminated system to construct a multiplicity, an effective totality, of the generative levels or mechanisms that you are concerned with. The fourth would be adherence to what I call the holy trinity of

59 Pilgrim D (2014) Understanding Mental Health: A critical realist exploration: Routledge

interdisciplinary research and this involves meta-theoretical unity, a methodological specificity, and a theoretical pluralism and tolerance.

Moving on, the fifth would be the removal of the huge career, social, financial, administrative barriers to interdisciplinary research; then we would be getting a science capable of dealing with open systemic phenomena.

There is much more to be said here, particularly about the moving away from what you have in the UK and many other societies, a two cultures world, moving to a world where someone whose prime orientation is in humanities or social sciences is also at home in the world of numbers and figures and vice versa, and that will involve educational changes.

The Critical Realist Embrace

By way of conclusion today I would like to sum up and talk about what I see as the advantages of critical realism. What critical realism aspires to be is, in short, maximally inclusive. Thus, for the critical realist everything is real, everything, which is a causal agent, is real. Thus, for a critical realist, beliefs, which are faults, are also, in virtue of being causally efficacious, real. For critical realists, language is real, mathematics is real, materiality is real; whatever has a causal effect is real and that gives a critical realist a maximally inclusive ontology.

At the same time, at an epistemological level, critical realists try to point out how, at different stages of the scientific process, different kinds of methods are called for, and how in relation to different objects of study, such as people on the one hand or molecules on the other, you will have different methods.

The first different stages could be illustrated by the DREI(C) model and, of course, the second could be illustrated by our acceptance of the absolute necessity for a hermeneutic moment in science, social science. That is the first advantage of critical realism.

The second advantage is that every other theory of science, or social science, or practice of critique, is susceptible to huge criticisms: these are either a priori, which are endemic to the philosophy, such as the problem induction is to empiricism and neo-Kantianism, or they are susceptible to criticisms that the critical realist can bring to bear on them, such as in the case of the idea that language is the only important thing to study in the social world – the social constructivist idea – is subject to huge critical realist critiques, turning round how do you have a language without reference? Is it possible to imagine meaning as just a relation between signifier and signified? No, the critical realist says, you have to have a reference, and that constitutes a huge critique of the social constructivist position, of the beginning of it.

Now, one particular form of criticism which I call Achilles' Heel[60] critique is very strong, where the criticism turns on the very point that the system of philosophy feels strongest in, so this might be like empiricism in relation to experimental activity. You might say, well, you know, you are against me everywhere else but here I am strong. Critical realism says no, that is where you are actually weakest and that is a very strong form of criticism.

---

60 It is what I have called the Achilles' Heel critique. In this form of critique you seize on the most important premise for a particular position and show how that premise and all the beautiful insights that are hoped to be sustained by it cannot in fact be sustained on the basis of that specified ontology, epistemology and methodology. It is a real blow to the empiricist, who believes that all knowledge about the world comes via constant conjunctions of experience, to realise that this cannot do justice to experimentally produced experience, which is the only sort of experience that the natural scientist is normally interested in. Likewise, it would be a blow to a Marxist, for example, if you could show on the basis of their epistemology that they cannot sustain the concept of class consciousness. It would be a blow to the hermeneuticists and social constructionists if you could show that they cannot sustain the intelligibility of language on their assumptions. So that is the Achilles' Heel critique, and it is the most powerful instrument for arriving at a more inclusive conceptual formation. Bhaskar in Bhaskar, R & Hartwig, M (2010: 79).

The third point to make here is that, extraordinarily, the actual other systems, insofar as they survive, insofar as they can cope with reality, have to use critical realism so that their practice is what I call a *TINA formation*.[61] It is a combination of a practice, which will make do in virtue of using an implicit critical realism and a false theory, which appears to steer it.

When you think about this, critical realism offers few adherents of such philosophies – a very inviting future because what we say is, I recognise your implicit practice, recognise what you are really doing to make this thing seem to work for you and when you recognise that, you will gradually throw off the false meta-theory and develop further in a more rationally self-conscious way the exciting nugget of truth in your theory.

So we say to everyone, in an age when if you study a social science you also study, inevitably, philosophy, become philosophically, methodologically self-conscious and choose to be extant before you begin your research or your investigation, a critical realist.

This is what I have called the *Critical Realist Embrace*.[62]

---

61 Basically, 'a truth in practice combined or held in tension with a falsity in theory', issuing in emergent error and illusion (Bhaskar 2012b 84-5)...named ironically for the British prime minister Thatcher's slogan, 'There is no alternative'. The intention is to show that there are, after all, alternatives. Hartwig M Ed (2007) TINA Syndrome, Dictionary of Critical Realism: Routledge

62 However, what critical realism tries to do is give a picture of the whole. This means that critical realists can embrace the insights of other positions and need not fear anything from them. Critical realists are welcome to join in, but so too are social constructionists, empiricists, neo-Kantians and

You do not have to actually be a critical realist to come on board; just come on board and if you think that language is the most important thing in the social world, welcome! You are welcome; we have no objection to anything positively you say. We would only have an objection if you try and stop someone else who thought that, say, class or inequality was the most important thing in the social world doing what he or she wanted to do.

It is a welcome to all to come on board, enjoy the critical realist embrace and we will learn and develop further by working with you. Because, of course, the last thing that a critical realist wants to say is that they have a monopoly of a truth or an interesting position. So there is much you can learn from non critical realists but I suggest critical realism will always be the meta-theory that you need to use to get the most out of these other systems and philosophies and thinkers.

any other variety of philosopher, social theorist and researcher. This could be called the critical realist embrace. Bhaskar in Bhaskar, R & Hartwig, M (2010: 78)

"[…] if emancipation is to be possible, well grounded explanations of false consciousness and more generally ill-being must be capable of informing self conscious transformative practice, unfettering human productive, developmental, life enhancing and consumptive powers and possibilities." Roy Bhaskar (2009: 242)

Chapter Two[63]

Duality

Dialectical Critical Realism

Live Stream took place 24th May 2014

---

63 (Ed) Roy was very unwell on the day of the live stream and I did wonder if we would be able to go ahead, but we did. Consequently, however, once I had created the YouTube video Roy did not want me to publish it. He felt that he was not able to fully explain DCR. It took much persuading of Roy that the talk was understandable. And in the end he agreed to let me publish the video. As I edited this talk I began to see the challenge Roy had in communicating the complexity of DCR, and at times, it does feel as if the text is starting to become very abstract. I have tried to liberate Roy's talk by added more footnotes to aid understanding. My recommendation when reading the text, is the same that Roy would offer, read the text, think about it, then come back and read it again, only holding on to as much as you need.

"What I argued was that dialectic[64] was a very rational process, characteristic of all learning and development. It is motivated and powered throughout negativity, by absence. What sets the dialectic going is some absence, such as in the human world a lack. You are hungry so you are driven to look for food. Then you try and to abolish or eliminate the constraints. In science you leave something out of your description of reality. Sooner or later that something you have left out will resurface in your description of reality and take the form of a contradiction." Roy Bhaskar (2012c: 129)

---

64 In Plato's Apology Socrates famously remarks, 'the unexamined life is not worth living'. The way Plato portrays it, the sort of examination Socrates has in mind is dialectical. The study and refinement of dialectic, in fact, became one of the central features of philosophical eduction in medieval and Renaissance thought. There is however no single, precise definition of dialectic. But in a nutshell, dialectical thinking may be thought of as a sort of philosophical dialogue – a back and forth process between two or more points of view. [...] dialectics is about discovering or disclosing truths not yet (or no longer) known. Baggini J & Fosl P (2010: 49)

Introduction and Levels of Ontology

Dialectical Critical Realism[65] (*and referred to as DCR*) is the second of the three main stages of critical realism: the first stage which we discussed in the last chapter, basic critical realism, consists of transcendental realism and the philosophy of science, critical naturalism as a philosophy of social science and the theory of dialectical critique as a sort of proto ethics.

Then we have dialectical critical realism and in the next chapter, I will be looking at the third stage, which is the philosophy of metaReality. The best way to see these three phases together is to see them as exercises in ontology as developing the arguments that we advanced last time.

You will remember when we began basic critical realism, we saw that it had begun with a double argument about ontology: an argument for ontology and against its reduction to epistemology and an argument against the implicit ontology of the dominant traditions in western philosophy; this implicit ontology we saw was actualist, which was of a kind which would have nature effectively either useless or impossible. What we are doing now in this chapter is developing ontology and in the next chapter take a deeper and more specified account of being.

---

65 (Ed) Dialectical Critical Realism (DCR) is perhaps the most complex and challenging stage of critical realism, I would therefore recommend beginning with Alderson P (2013:48-71) 12 Main Concepts in DCR, in which Alderson offers a very sound overview of DCR. Then move on to Norrie A (2010) Dialectics and Difference. Norrie offers an excellent deep introduction to both Dialectical Critical Realism and the DCR texts.

What we got from basic critical realism was, you might say, an idea of being as such and an exploration of being as involving non-identity. Two particular forms of non-identity [66] came very much to the fore: differentiation and stratification, that was the main thrust of the ontology we developed last time. Actually, of course, we need and we need philosophically to know much more about the world than that it is differentiated, say between open and closed systems, and stratified, say between generative mechanisms and structures on the one hand and events on the other or between the domains of the real and the actual.

This deepening ontology is what dialectical critical realism and the philosophy of metaReality achieves.

What I am going to do now is just list the seven levels of ontology that we will be exploring together:

- **The first level (1M) is a level, which thinks or understands being as such and being as non-identity.**
- **The second level, (2E), explores being as process, being as involving negativity, change and absence.**
- **The third level (3L) explores being as together as internally related and as a whole.**
- **The fourth level (4D) understands being as incorporating transformative praxis.**

Those are the four levels of Dialectical Critical Realism.

---

66 (Ed) Think of non-identity as not the same as. So ontology is not the same as epistemology, the real is not the same as the actual.

In the next talk, we will be discussing the three further levels of the philosophy of metaReality:

- **The fifth level, (5A), understands being as reflexive and generally interior.**
- **The sixth level, called (6R) understands being as being re enchantment.**
- **The seventh level (7Z) understands being as incorporating the primacy of identity over difference and unity over split and in particular understands being as non-duality.**

Of the four levels of DCR that I will be concentrating on in this talk, basic critical realism has said a little bit about the first level at 1M, and a little bit about the fourth level, 4D.

The philosophy of science has talked about structure and difference, (1M), and the philosophy of social science of critical realism has talked about social concepts of transformative agency and structure (4D) so we have already got some components of dialectical critical realism there.

However, dialectical critical realism which I suppose was initiated with the publication of my book, *Dialectic: The Pulse of Freedom*[67] in 1993 and then *Plato ETC,*[68] a year later, is a systematic deepening of all the four

67 Dialectic: The Pulse of Freedom (2008b) Routledge

68 Plato ECT. (2010) Routledge.

levels and what I want to do in this talk is to go through the main features of those four levels

So, I will just repeat the four levels for you:

1M	Understands being as such and being as non-identity.
2E	Involves being as a process as incorporating change and negativity.
3L	Being as internally related as a whole.
4D	Emphasises being as incorporating transformative praxis.

Table Three: MELD

MELD[69]

1M – First Moment – Non Identity[70]

Starting with 1M; almost all the developments reported in basic critical realism involve relations of non-identity and that is why it is a key feature of 1M; we say that the transitive and the intransitive dimensions are distinct. That ontology is something which is not the same as epistemology, cannot be reduced to it, that the domain of the real; talking about causal rules and fields and structures cannot be reduced to, i.e., is not the same as, patterns of events. Patterns of events are not the same as our experiences, so we have the differences between domains of the real, the actual and the empirical.

---

69 Sketching the movement in his thinking, Bhaskar refers to these four elements in his dialectic as involving a 'first moment' (non-identity), a 'second edge' (negativity), a 'third level' (totality) and a 'fourth dimension' (ethical agency). He then abbreviates these elements as 1M, 2E, 3L and 4D, giving rise to the shorthand of the 'MELD' schema. Norrie A (2010: 3 n2)

70 1M=Prime (first) moment. Characterized by non-identity relations, such as those involved in the critique of the epistemic and anthropic fallacies, of identity theory and actualism. Unified by the concept of alterity, it emphasizes existential intransitivity, referential detachment, the reality principle and ontology which it necessitates. More concretely, it fastens on to the transcendentally necessary stratification and differentiation of the world, entailing concepts of causal powers and generative mechanisms, alethic truth and transfactuality, natural necessity and natural kinds. Bhaskar (2008b: 392)

	Domain of the Real	Domain of the Actual	Domain of the Empirical
Mechanisms	✓		
Events	✓	✓	
Experiences	✓	✓	✓

Figure Six: The Domains

In the corpus of dialectical critical realism, we move on quite a bit further. Two very general points about ontology need to be noted: the first that ontology is explicitly thematised as all inclusive, so ontology includes knowledge, it includes epistemology, but it includes also error and illusion and illusion can have a causal effect and we say that in general anything that has a causal effect, or causal power, is real. So ontology will include mathematical mistakes for instance; ontology is all inclusive.[71]

Then ontology is also inexorable because there is no way you cannot do ontology if you give an account of knowledge or an account of language then you are implicitly giving an account of the world known in knowledge or spoken about in the language. So, you cannot help but do ontology.

Then we specify a particular objects, topics, that need a realist analysis so we have dispositional realism, this is the idea that possibilities are real not just actualities. If we have an actuality, something has

---

71 (Ed) If you ask someone to talk about something, then there is a some-THING that is being talked about, even if the person only speaks of their feelings about the some-thing, the some-thing is still there. The some-thing is still having effect.

happened, then the possibility is actualises or realises must also be real and in general, that possibility, it sits along with a possibility of different things.

The idea that another world is possible or a better world or the idea that we can consciously move towards it all be it of things which is situated by dispositional realism, this becomes very important in what I call concrete utopians.

Then another form of realism (all of these realisms are implied by the necessary or the dialectical development of transcendental realism) is categorical realism. This is the idea that the categories, the objects that philosophers like to talk about, like causality, law, they themselves are real, they are not as Kant and Popper for instance would have them, subjective impositions that we put on the world, rather they are in reality itself. So the world contains not only lots of different causal laws it contains causality, law, etc as such.

The Semiotic Triangle[72]

A very important extension of realism here comes in the theory of meaning and the crucial concept here is the semiotic triangle. The semiotic triangle is a triangle with its three apexes constituted by the signifier, which is the word or symbol, the signified, which is the meaning or concept, and thirdly the referent, which is the object to which the signifier refers. Typically in Saussurean[73] and Post-Saussurean semiotics, analysis of meaning of language, the referent is dropped so we just have a relationship between the signifier and the signified; in fact, it can be a very complex relationship of the sort that someone like Derrida[74] will analyse but there is no referent there.

---

72 Critical realism provides a resolution to the (communicative) interactionism-instrumentalism problem with the Bhaskarian idea of (1) referential detachment, an argument parallel to the revindication of ontology and Bhaskar's (2) semiotic triangle. Both (1) and (2) help us to resolve the (communicative) interactionism-instrumentalism dichotomy because, without collapsing reality into dualisms, it allows us to understand the triad of relations among: the realm of communication that includes language in broad terms or what in the semiotic triangle is denoted as signifier, the realm of epistemology, the objects and methods of knowledge, or what in the semiotic triangle is denoted as signified, and the realm of ontology, the referents which are the external and real objects of science, such that these objects are detached from the other two realms. A problem could arise, for example, if language is detached from this communication–activity link, in which case, we fall into a postmodernist perspective, the view of reality is exhausted by concepts, as if language appears to enslave the individual in 'the prison-house of language' Following the critical realist semiotic triangle, to refer raises the possibility of opening a debate about some referent, something in the world[...] Nunez I (2014: 53)

73 Ferdinand Mongin de Saussure (November 1857 – February 1913)

74 Jacques Derrida (July 1930 – October 2004)

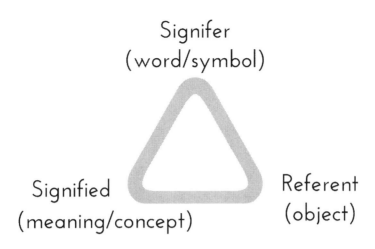

Signifer
(word/symbol)

Signified
(meaning/concept)

Referent
(object)

Figure Seven: The Semiotic Triangle

Without a referent the whole point of language, which is to enable us to coherently steer our way around the world, is lost. I should just add that the Anglo Saxon and the American tradition, being linguistics has often made the opposite mistake of assuming a single relationship between signifier and referent so that the signified, the concept, the meaning, gets lost.

We need to clearly situate language in a world, a world which exists in large part independently of the uses of that language and so it is situated in the context or the semiotic triangle and the world in which things have become referentially detached from the language we use to describe it, this is the important concept: referential detachment.[75]

---

75 Referential detachment begins life as a concept associated with the relationship between knowledge and being. The initial idea is, in brief, that any act of knowing involves an ontological commitment to separate the knower from the known, to detach the referrer from the referent. Norrie. A (2010:140)

Truth Tetrapolity[76]

and

Emancipatory Discourse[77]

Then we have here an alethic realism, a realism about truth. Dialectical critical realism argues that philosophers had a too simple concept of truth and actually what is involved in the concept of truth are four distinct components.

The first component could be called the **fiduciary component** *(normative-fiduciary)*: this is the sense of true which is involved when you say 'this is true' and we mean trust me, take my word for it. This is truth as a social bond.

---

76 [...]we should note here that truth talk about the (moral) world has four different elements. It is, first, 'normative-fiduciary', meaning that it is communicative in the sense of saying 'trust me – act on it'. Second, it is 'adequating', meaning it provides an epistemic sense of what is 'warrantedly assertable' – that is, what may reasonably be said about the world. Third, it is 'referential-expressive', meaning that it links what is asserted epistemically in the transitive to the intransitive dimension of knowledge. Fourth, it is alethic, in that it accesses 'the truth of or reason for things and phenomena, not propositions, as genuinely ontological, and in this sense as objective in the intransitive dimension' (Bhaskar 2008b: 217). These four elements Bhaskar calls the 'truth tetrapolity'. Norrie A (2010: 128)

77 Emancipatory discourse is so common to all human aspirations. Consider western liberal through. Let us take Rousseau. Rousseau says man is born free but is everywhere in chains, so immediately he says that man's essential nature is to be free, but something happens when he or she grows up and the become imprisoned on chains. That is society. Bhaskar (2012c: 135)

Then we have secondly the more assertible evidential sense of **truth (*adequating*),** this is the sense in which we say that something is true when we have sufficient evidence to assert it in a scientific context. And that of course is the complex truth that most philosophers have concentrated on.

Thirdly, there is a very interesting sense of concept of true which I call the ***expressive-referential.*** This is the sense in which the grass is green, perfectly expressive - the greenness of grass - and we can understand the grass is green as straddling the ontic/epistemic divide.

The fourth sense of **true (*alethic*)**[78] is a genuinely fully ontological sense of true in which I might want to say something like the truth of the fact that water boils at a 100° centigrade lies in its molecular constitution. In other words, here I am saying the truth at one level of reality is the structure that produces it at a higher order of reality, and ontological stratification and alethic truth sit side by side.

---

78 Alethic truth, as optimally grounding reason, can be the rational cause of transformative negating agency in absenting constraints on self-emancipation, that is, on the liberation of our causal powers to flourish. For to exist is to be able to become, which is to possess the capacity for self-development, a capacity that can be fully realized only in a society founded on the principle of universal concretely singularized human autonomy in nature. This process is dialectic; and it is the pulse of freedom. Bhaskar. (2008b: 385)

Normative-Fiduciary	Trust me – Act on it
Adequating	What may reasonably be said about the world.
Referential-Expressive	Links what is asserted epistemically in the transitive to the intransitive dimension of knowledge.
Alethic	The truth of or reason for things and phenomena, not propositions, as genuinely ontological.

Table Four: Truth Tetrapolity

Another important concept, which is given a realist interpretation in dialectical critical realism, is that of a *TINA formation*.[79] A TINA formation occurs when it is falsity in theory is combined with the truth in practice. The sort of thing I am thinking of here, for example, could be illustrated by the way in which chemists and physicists observe in practice a distinction between open and closed systems. However, they do not regard the open systemic world as quantifying their experimentally

---

79 The Tina syndrome is important for Bhaskar, for his general view is that the history of western philosophy from Plato onwards represents a series of Tina compromise formations, and he thinks that specific episodes in philosophy can be seen as exercises in Tina thinking. Taking general history first, what is lacking throughout western philosophy, he argues, is a proper understanding of the polyvalent (to include absence) quality of ontology, and the import of natural necessity for being in the world. In place of a sufficiently realist ontology, an emphasis on the role of knowledge over being (the epistemic fallacy) and a corresponding flat, actualist and monovalent, ontology are established. The coexistence in epistemology of the epistemic fallacy with an actualist (no depth), monovalent (no absence) ontology represents a bar on the philosophical understanding of both knowledge and being that moves from Plato and Aristotle to Descartes and Hume, then on to Kant and Hegel and up to the present. Norrie A. (2010:107)

generated results. At the same time they feel that they can use the results of a careful experimental work to make statements about how the world is going on transfactuality quite independently of the closure or otherwise of the systems.

You would not be a chemist, you would not be a physicist unless you observe that distinction in practice, but of course that would sit very uneasily with the empiricist theory the empirical realist adopt. And so there will be an uneasy compromise formations in which they carry on successfully doing the right thing but cannot think why it is the right thing, so that you have this theory and practice inconsistencies and the TINA formation is the typical mechanism in which the illusions and ideological errors under which we live is reproduced.[80]

Then, finally, I want to point to a basic logic, which can be brought out clearly here at our 1M. This is the logic of emancipatory discourse. When a theory articulates the possibilities of freedom, what it will be often typically be doing is positing a basic level of human being

---

80 An example is the TINA argument that schooling must be compulsory. In England, this supports policies to make school attendance compulsory up to 18 years of age, 'truancy sweeps' by the police, fines and imprisonment for parents whose children miss school, and deeply held TINA assumptions that many children have to be forced and punished into learning. This can result in alienated students feeling 'separated, split, torn and estranged from oneself, or what is essential and intrinsic to one's nature or identity ... to be alienated is to lose part of one's autonomy' (Bhaskar 2008b: 114) in the 'dialectic of malaise' (Bhaskar 2008b: 287) in one's knowing and being on all four planes of social being. The alternative would be to reconsider the natural necessity of young children's avid learning and how schools could nurture this more fully through the dialectic of equity and de-alienation (Bhaskar 2008b: 287–92) to avoid the splits and alienation in education, explored in great detail, for example, by John Holt (1964) and many others. Alderson P (2013:114)

which, of course, sustains another level which has become emergent from it which is also acting as a constraint. Thus, you might have human capacity to labour being constrained in Marxist theory by the existence of class relations. The argument is that at a certain point, the capacity to labour, will break free, throw off the level which is emergent and sitting on it and fettering those basic human productive forces.[81] Which is a very familiar pattern: there is a level of the human being, an activity which is productive, which contributes to human happiness And then there is another level which is fettering it and this other level is emergent from the more basic level and what is required is an act of dissonance for it to be shed.

There is an ontological a-symmetry here because the arguments of the person committed to the logic of the emancipatory discourse would be that we cannot have a society which human beings do not create, are not productive, but we can have a society without exploitative class relations. Those are some of the developments under 1M.

---

81 In Marx and Rousseau, there is at some level a notion that human beings are all right. If you take the case of Marx, human beings work, working is very important to human beings and they work and they improve their existence. But of course in the Marxian model, the productive forces are constrained by the class structure, and so what you have to do to liberate these productive forces is to transform the class structure, that is you have to get rid of classes. So, what's involved is a dis-emergence , a shedding. This seems to be an important thing that we have to do generally in life. We might start smoking at one stage and then we have to give up smoking to improve our existence. Bhaskar (in Scott D 2015: 37)

2E- Second Edge [82]- Absence

Now 2E, which is properly within dialectical critical realism, this is the most important of the levels and it is the level, which requires a new or considerably developed philosophical system.

So, let us focus on the concept of change. When you say that something changes what you are saying is that something which was there has passed out of existence and/or something that was there has come into being. In either case, you are involved with negativity and with absence[83], with the disappearance of what was or the appearance from what was not of something new.

This is our normal everyday understanding of change and this was pronounced by Parmenides[84] in Ancient Greek times as being absolutely

---

82 2E=Second edge. Unified by the category of absence, from which the whole circuit of 1M-4D links and relations can be derived, its critical cutting edge is aimed at the Parmenidean doctrine of ontological monovalance, the Platonic analysis of negation and change in terms of difference and the Kantian analysis of negative into positive predicates. It spans the gamut of categories of negativity, contradiction and critique. Bhaskar (2008b: 392)

83 At the core of Dialectic is the concept of absence. Introduced early in the book, in discussing 'negation', it is the springboard for developing critical realism by providing a 'second edge' (2E) based on an understanding of 'absence' or 'negativity'. 'Absence' is, however, the term given central place in dialectical critical realism, for dialectic involves, at its most complete, 'the absenting of constraints on the absenting of absences, or ills' (Bhaskar 2008b: 396). This formula sometimes feels slightly strained; we are not used to speaking of absence in quite this way, and we do not usually think of dialectic in terms of this kind of language. Norrie A. (2010: 23)

84 But Parmenides also bequeathed another legacy to philosophy: the generation of a purely positive, complementing a purely actual, notion of reality, in what I am going to nominate the doctrine of ontological monovalence. In this study I aim to revindicate negativity. Indeed, by the

wrong. He said, in effect, you cannot have change in the real world and this is of course a striking doctrine because it seems obvious that there appears to be change. Now his doctrine of what I call ontological monovalence [85] prohibiting ontological change has proved profoundly important and ontological monovalence [86] together with the epistemic fallacy and actualism are the three unholy errors of Western philosophy [87].

Had Parmenides just left it at that of course and no one followed up it might have been regarded as a typically philosophical statement. And it is due to Plato that this parmenidean idea became received doctrine.

What Plato did was he analysed a apparent change in terms of difference and in a substantive scientific way this is supported by an idea that what happened when something seemed to change whilst not really

---

time we are through, I would like the reader to see the positive as a tiny, but important, ripple on the surface of a sea of negativity. Bhaskar (2008b: 4)

85 (Ed) The view that whatever exists must have always existed and cannot change or cease to exists.

86 [...]we see the re-vindication of the notion of negativity and with it the very important critique of ontological monovalence: 'the generation of a purely positive to complement a purely actual notion of reality', (Bhaskar 2008b: 5) a concept that has determined the course of Western philosophy. Nunez, I (2014: xi). Also see Norrie (2010: 42) Ontological monovalence in western philosophy

87 Back to the unholy trinity. As ontological monovalence, taken literally, entails the exclusion of alterity, otherness, it implies, as primeval monism, the identity of thought and being, whether this takes the form of the epistemic fallacy or the ontic fallacy. I shall later argue for the historical primacy of the former from Plato, following in fact Parmenides. But in any event we have the ordering: ontological monovalence → epistemic fallacy → primal squeeze (Ed concepts of understanding reality are squeeze out: such as ontological stratification) Bhaskar (2010: 45)

change but just a redistribution of unchanging parts. So these unchanging parts might be forms in Plato[88] or they might be atoms in atomism[89].

This idea that you can understand change along the lines of difference of course denies the difference between saying that Sophie's hair colour on Tuesday is different from Sophie's hair colour today and saying that Sophie dyed her hair. Sophie changed the colour of her hair or the colour of her hair changed, because what is involved in the talking of change is the idea of an underlying continuum, a substance which remained unchanged, which underwent the transformation and this may not be simply a substance it could be a region of spatial time so that one can say that the difference between saying that in this café we have Sartre and we do not have Pierre and saying that in this café Sartre greeted the arrival of Pierre is understood in terms of a change in state, then with the arrival of Pierre.[90]

---

88 See Form entry in Proudfoot M, & Lacey AR (2009: 142) The Routledge Dictionary of Philosophy, Routledge

89 See Atomism entry in Proudfoot M, & Lacey AR (2009: 27) The Routledge Dictionary of Philosophy, Routledge

90 If I say, 'Sophie was dyeing her hair on Wednesday', I refer 'to a process of substantial change which cannot be captured by the formal difference between the statement that her hair was grey [on Tuesday], but brown [on Thursday]' (Bhaskar 2010: 8). To speak of change is to invoke the absenting or determinate negation of a past state. A past state is absented by changes that occur in causally constituting the present, and absenting and change are essential to our understanding of being over time. It is crucial to our ability to understand the way the world works that a statement concerning change is distinct from one concerning difference, for the latter can tell us something, but not all that we would want to know, about a situation of change. Change entails difference but is not reducible to it. For example, to return to the example from Sartre in Chapter 2, the change

So the analysis of change that dialectical critical realism put forward is consistent with our ordinary and complex change and involves a view in which the cosmos in which we see emergence or the production of new things as being a vital feature.

Now, how would you convince yourself that the DCR analysis was right? Well, one way of doing it is to think about ontological change and epistemological change.

You might see there is a difference between you saying that it started to rain in Manchester, which is about Manchester, and my saying Jack believes that it rains in Manchester, or it is correct to say that it is raining in Manchester.[91]

In one case the absenting, the negation, is in the world itself and in the other case it is in our description of the world. For DCR we can have change but, of course, unless epistemic change was also ontological

---

constituted by Pierre's absence from his chair in the café is not explained by noting the difference constituted by Genet having taken his place. It may be related to the additional, causally efficacious fact that Pierre has gone off to play football, rather than waiting to meet Sartre" Norrie A (2010: 162)

91 (Ed) I find this passage of the text the most challenging to understand, so It might help if I offer an explanation here; recall that change means absence or negation, so to say that it is raining in Manchester is to also implies the possibility of it not raining or there is an absence of rain in Manchester, which of course is about the world. Rain being (Ontological) in the world. Saying that Jack believes it is raining in Manchester or that it is correct to say it is raining in Manchester, implies the absenting or negation, the absenting of absenting of "I know that it is not raining in Manchester" or Jack believes that it is not raining in Manchester, both are negations, or absence of knowing or beliefs about the world (Epistemological).

change we would not have language, beliefs and knowledge in the world of itself as properties of the world.[92]

Therefore, what DCR puts at the centre of our attention is the idea of determinant absences. It is not concerned with nothingness in determinant absence, it is concerned with things like the absence of rain or some concrete instance of something not happening which has a causal effect and which we need to take account of in our understanding of reality.

---

92 Absence is not only necessary for being, but change, properly understood, presupposes absence, i.e. the coming into being of new properties or entities and the passing away from being of previously existing ones. Absence yields not only the clue to the vexed problem of dialectic, which may be seen as depending on the rectification of absence (omissions, incompleteness) in a move to greater generality, inclusiveness and coherence, but is necessary for a full understanding of intentional action. Bhaskar, in Bhaskar et al (2010: 15)

Marx[93], Hegel[94] and Dialectics

I would like to say a little bit about a 2E notion, which many are very mystified about, and namely the idea of dialectics. I can start it best by going back to Marx's famous research on Hegel's dialectic. You may recall that Marx's wrote to Engel that Hegel had discovered the secret of all knowledge. The scientific method in his elucidation of his dialectic, and that if he had a bit more time he would like nothing better than to write a couple of printed sheets explaining what this secret of the scientific method was.[95]

Well, it is very unfortunate he did not do this and many other people since then have tried to explain what they consider the secrets of dialectic is. One gentleman in the nineteenth century wrote a book called the Secrets of Hegel,[96] and after three or four hundred pages, one could say the reader would be no wiser as to what this was.

Well actually, I think that dialectic is a complex concept and there are many different kinds of dialectics, which in DCR I try and defract, separate out, and reconstruct.

---

93 Karl Marx (May 1818 – March 1883)

94 Georg Wilhelm Friedrich Hegel (August 1770 – November 1831)

95 Unfortunately Marx never consummated his somewhat whimsical wish—'to make accessible to the ordinary human intelligence, in two or three printers' sheets, what is rational in the method which Hegel discovered and at the same time mystified. Bhaskar (2008b: 87)

96 The Secret of Hegel: Being the Hegelian System in Origin Principle, Form and Matter: James Hutchison Stirling 1865

But it is quite clear that there is one kind of dialectic, which is the one that excited Marx and I think DCR can give a very simple and plausible explanation of this. Let us go back to science and Kuhn's description of science in terms of "normal science" in which the scientist is a neophyte who is being trained, is tested, and then "revolutionary science" in which concepts are being radically transformed.[97]

I think it has got to be a very simple dialectical critical realist reconstruction of the different phases of science. Any theory will try and describe all the causally relevant factors or impinging on the result that is it is described. Very often, and in fact you could say pretty much it always tends to be the case, scientists will not succeed in doing that. Although the attempt is being made to describe a whole field, something causally relevant has been left out and sooner or later the causally relevant thing that has been left out will extract its toll on the theory. The incompleteness will generate inconsistencies and contradictions, which will appear to the theorist as a signalling device that they have left something out.

---

97 Looking at a contour map, the student sees lines on paper, the cartographer a picture of a terrain. Looking at a bubble-chamber photograph, the student sees confused and broken lines, the physicist a record of familiar sub-nuclear events. Only after a number of such transformations of vision, does the student become an inhabitant of the scientist's world, seeing what the scientist sees and responding as the scientist does. The world that the student then enters is not, however, fixed once and for all by the nature of the environment, on the one hand, and of science, on the other. Rather, it is determined jointly by the environment and the particular normal-scientific tradition that the student has been trained to pursue. Therefore, at times of revolution, when the normal-scientific tradition changes, the scientist's perception of his environment must be re-educated—in some familiar situations he must learn to see a new gestalt. Kuhn (2012: 112)

Of course, what scientist have left out very often in science is something they did not know about and so what this situation of tremendous contradictions yields, in pre-revolutionary situations is revolutionary situations, in which a new concept has to be there to restore scientific equilibrium.

From a realist standpoint, or a meta-standpoint that means, something new has to be discovered about the world but you have to discover what it is that has been left out, of course, in Newton's case it was what caused gravity;[98] when Einstein formulated the special theory of relativity it was that he discovered what Newton had left out[99].

After the discovery then consistency in the conceptual field can be restored, thus there is a simple way of describing a dialectic of scientific knowledge in which an absence or an incompleteness in the theory generates, leads to, contradictions and other aporia[100] or problems which proliferate, necessitating the discovery of what it is that has been left out and that is a scientific breakthrough or a scientific revolution. This is a very simple and plausible process that occurs in science.

Could we say something more general might occurring in society? Well, in the couple of decades before the First World War, in the 19th century, we had the phenomenon of the suffragette movement,

---

98 (Ed) Isaac Newton noted that; gravity must be caused by an agent acting constantly according to certain laws, but whether this agent be material or immaterial I have left to the consideration of my readers Newton I (1692/3) Letters to Bentley

99 (Ed) In 1915, Albert Einstein imagined an agent that caused gravity. According to his theory of General Relativity, gravity is a natural consequence of a mass's influence on space.

100 (Ed) A philosophical puzzle or state of puzzlement.

and what was the suffragette movement about, it was about the huge incompleteness, absence, in the political field that women could not vote. In the course of those decades, the decade or so after it, women in the western world at least were granted the suffrage so that what had happened is the political totality had been transformed to be a more inclusive one. The absence had been remedied or rectified. This of course proved a problem for many countries in the western world in the 20s and 30s and particularly the colonial powers in Europe: that they were the masters of colonial peoples who were denied their own democratic rights and denied the right to be self-determining in respect of their own countries.

Again, we can see how this necessitated a response to this challenge and causal pressures that it brought to bear, that were brought to bear on the political setup in those powers and until you had a state of decolonisation and then of course the argument can be taken further.

You can argue was this decolonisation real or purely formal, and then you can take the argument into the field of democracy. So we can say ok, we have the vote, but how responsive are our political leaders to our needs and wants and our best interest and would not there be a way of improving the democracy we have, and so the arguments continue.

What is important to note is that there is a clear mechanism in such a dialectical process, a clear learning mechanism in which our response to a social situation or problem, moves in a negentropic way, that moves to increasing order, and that negentropy is very well stated, by Hegel.

We can now make sense of the Marxist metaphor of the kernel in the mystical shell and say the rational kernel of dialectic, or at least that kind of epistemological way of dialectic, is the remedy of incompleteness or absence by building a greater, more inclusive, more comprehensive totality of theoretical or social thoughts.

There is quite a lot more that could be said about dialecticism, I will not say it here, only that you have had enough to whet your appetite to read it in the DCR texts.[101]

There is another 2E concept that is very important to note and that is in 2E we theorise in a critical realist way, space time and tense and in particular a useful concept is that of a rhythmic which is a spatio-temporality causal process.[102] What is intimated by this concept is the tri-unity and irreducibility of geography, history and social theory. The concept of the past and future are also given deeper readings, if you just look around the room that you are in you will note where the furniture comes from and when roughly the house or the building that you are in was constructed.

Then when you think about the philosophical ideas that you are talking about, you are talking about philosophical ideas like actualism, like

101 Dialectic: The Pulse of Freedom (2008b) Routledge and Plato ECT. (2010) Routledge.

102 Everything is also tensed in being largely constituted by its past and geo-history, and it exists through many overlapping, converging or contradicting rhythmics. Bhaskar describes these rhythmics in great cities where buildings, ceremonies, conflicts, 'electric cables, motor cars, television sets, rickshaws, scavengers and disposable cans coalesce in a locale'. Space, time, cause, structure and agency all interact as product-in-process, process-in-product. Alderson P. (2013: 110)

ontological monovalence, which had been wrongly handed down, and you can say that to a large extent we are living the presence of the past.

3L – Third Level [103] – Totality [104]

3L is very important: it is the level in which we explore not taking things extensively, not regarding things as atomistic and on there own but as together. That what I am saying now has to be taken with what I said in the last talk, and this particular sentence has to be related to the sentence before it, so they cannot be taken alone, they do not make sense alone. If you thought about relations in the family when we get a good sense of what one means by internal relations, [105] and so social relations and a lot of natural relations are external.

---

103 3L=Third level. Unified by the category of totality, it pinpoints the error of ontological extensionalism, including the hypostatization of thought. It encompasses such categories and themes as reflexivity, emergence, constellationality, holistic causality, internal relationality and intra-activity, but also detotalization, alienation, split and split-off, illicit fusion and fission. Its dialectics are of centre and periphery, form and content, figure and ground, generative separation and de-alienation, retotalization in a unity-indiversity. Its metacritics pivot on the identification of detotalization. There is a special affinity with 1M, since totality is a structure. Bhaskar (2008b: 392)

104 (Ed) Michael Bhaskar's, The Place of Totality in Dialectical Critical Realism, Journal of Critical Realism (2013 v12 :202 - 209) was originally presented to Roy Bhaskar's postgraduate critical realism reading group seminar at the Institute of Education, London, in 2012, the paper explores the concept of totality and is highly recommended reading to support the understanding of 3L and totality.

105 Some examples can help illustrate this. One offered in Dialectic The Pulse of Freedom (DFP) is a book - the text inside it is 'an internal related totality' the book seats on a library shelf, which is part of the totality of the books in the library and moreover the book itself forms a totality of the books used in its creation. In DPF we get the magisterial description of a range of totalities: the element of language, the ebb and flow of conversation, the sequential "habitus" of routine, the systemic independencies of the global monetary system, at play, a sculpture, or an experimental project orientated to the demediation of nature. Bhaskar M, (2013: 204)

The difference that this cup of tea does not make any difference to what is inside this bottle of water but my sitting here and talking to you is internally related to your interest and presence. So the idea of the internal relation is the arch idea in 3L and clearly we can move from take things together to taking things as a whole, as a totality.[106] In the social world most totalities are partial totality that is their totality is shot through by external relations as well as internal relations.

The concept of holistic causality is tremendously important and we will all be aware of it intuitively by the idea of a sense of component parts all of which interact so they produce a whole, and a whole, which in turn produces an effect on component parts. So that you have a complex of continuing interaction between parts and parts, parts and a whole, and whole and parts. A very important concept at 3L is that of a concrete[107] universal.[108]

---

106 Let us begin with two basic questions. First, why should we think in terms of totality at all? A general answer can be drawn from what we have seen so far. The idea of totality is necessitated by the nature of the natural and social worlds. If we think of spatio-temporal causality as central to human life, then human beings are caught in a structured flow of being and becoming in which the totality of past, present and future relations is implicated. If we think of dialectics as diffracted, we need to think of the grounds of diffraction, and how the whole is to be understood. Added to these general points, Bhaskar gives some examples from everyday life to illustrate why a sense of totality is central to being. To think of a language, a sentence, a text, a book or even a word is to think of entities where one has to grasp something as a whole as well as in its individual parts. [...] Norrie A. (2010: 88)

107 What does it mean to call something 'concrete'? We can get two purchases on this. First, it really makes sense only in contrast to its co-relative—'abstract' . Secondly, insofar as it has a

Most of the universals that western philosophy talks about are abstract universals. The idea here is that what you can say meaningfully and scientifically about something you should be able to say about all instances of that thing; so what we can say about a pen at a scientific and meaningful level I should be able to say about all pens. Now, of course that breaks down in the real world, I do not know of a single abstract universal. If you take something, which is universal, like a human being, you will find that human beings are all very different. Each human being will have what we call mediations, these are specified like sex or gender, its occupation, whether it is a parent, children, brother and sisters, whether it is a fan of The Rolling Stones or whatever, those are its mediations.

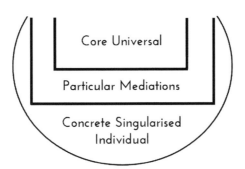

Figure Eight: The Concrete Singularity of the Human Agent

---

positive meaning of its own, its nearest synonym might be 'well-rounded', in the sense of balanced, appropriate and complete for the purposes at hand. Bhaskar (2008b: 128)

108 Concrete universality has to be seen in the context of stratification, spatio-temporal processualisation, totality and mediatedness, and in the light of the effects of negativity. All these elements give to the individual as a universal a sense of the real singularity that exists in the world, for in this processing of individuality, individuals are inseparable from the effects of real change and difference. Norrie A. (2010: 114)

Then supposing we focus onto women: we have exactly the same mediations when two women will themselves differ by having a different space-time path, one will be 35 and born in Goa, the other will be 70 and born in Timbuktu. That is our specific geo-historical trajectory of the particular instances of universal.

Now suppose we have two women who have exactly the same mediations and exactly the same geo-historical trajectory, they would nevertheless still be irreducibly different; they would have an irreducible uniqueness to them, they would be what we call 'concrete singularity.'[109] The theory of the concrete universal/concrete singular[110] is an important way in which dialectical critical realism makes it possible to identify real historical geo-historical individuals and talk about them.

Finally, I should note here the useful concept of a constellation.[111] We can think of, as I said earlier our knowledge is also part of being, so

---

109 This version of the concrete universal as concrete singular also has significant implications for how we think ethically about human being. The concrete singular as an individual 'consists in a core species-being, [and] particular mediations and rhythmics, uniquely individuating her or him as in effect a natural kind sui generis. Norrie A. (2010: 117)

110 Further, the idea of the concrete universal-singular not only stresses the spatio-temporal thrownness of each person, but also provides the basis for an ethical understanding of the uniqueness of each individual as a concrete singular being. Norrie A. (2010: 219)

111 The characteristic of constellationality is a key part of 3L: totality. There are two important notions to keep in mind when speaking about constellationality, (1) mediation, i.e., the means or medium of connection; and (2) what Alan Norrie calls 'differentia', as disconnection, or another way to say the difference between distinct, but overlapping levels of reality. For instance, constellationality is used to articulate traditional problems of opposition in terms of relations of

we can think of epistemology and knowledge as being contained or overreached by being and at the same time the knowledge will always have a specific intransitive object, that is a specific part of being would be what the knowledge is about. In this way, through this kind of figure of constellational overreaching containment, we can do justice to the sense in which ontology or being includes everything, including epistemology and knowledge and the sense in which knowledge and epistemology have specific intransitive objects.

---

containment. Such relations of containment mean that one term is contained as a subset of the other and that both terms make up a constellational unit. Nunez I (2014: 28)

4D- Fourth Dimension – Transformative Praxis [112]

Very briefly, then 4D. DCR has started by noticing the irreducibility of agency. When you think about it there is no way you cannot intend, intentionality is irreducible. And then, if you think about it, spontaneity or an immediate manifestation of thought in action is irreducible; at certain point, thought becomes action, there must be an element of spontaneity or as I think about next time, when we discuss the philosophy of metaReality, non-duality for agency to be possible at all.

We saw last time how the concept of the transformation model of the social activity which specifies relations between structure and agency needs to be expanded to the concept of four-planer social being. This is the idea that everything that occurs in society, the social world, occurs simultaneously at four different levels: the level of material transactions in nature, the level of social interactions between people, the level of social structure, and the level of stratification of the embodied personality.

---

112 Now, we can think of 4D: transformative praxis, as the point of introducing dialectic of freedom, i.e., the desire to be desired and this involves the desire to be recognized, again through the logic of dialectical universalizing insofar as this involves the capacity to enjoy rights and liberties, [it] entails the real enjoyment of equal and universally reciprocally recognized rights and liberties, including the right to de-alienation and the enjoyment of health, education, access to resources and liberties. Thus, we see that 4D: transformative praxis entails that emancipation must be grounded on self-authority; hence it needs to be self-emancipation such that we cannot emancipate a group of workers under the flag of a revolutionary working class. People themselves are self-revolutions, i.e., each individual has to create conditions as an emancipatory agent. Nunez I (2014: 63)

Now one of the problems that the Left in particular has to face is that projects to orientate social change have in general only been directed to the transformation in social structure, whereas to change our social lives, to change society, we need to operate on all four levels.

By the same token it can be said that the Right generally has restricted itself to, or tendencies within it, to self-improvement, to the improvements of the level of stratification of the embodied personality.

Of course, we need action on all these fronts for genuine and social change to occur.

Ethics

The development of critical realism is itself dialectical in that what it is trying to do is to remedy an absence in the pre-critical realist theme and also remedy an incompleteness or absence in its own previous exposition. If we start at the beginning of basic critical realism this was very concerned to remedy the absence of ontology in the existing discursive situation, and that we had an ontology in transcendental realism for naturalism. And then in critical naturalism, this was developed further on to an ontology for social science, remedying the incompleteness there. Similarly, at the level of the explanatory critique we were developing a theory of ethics.

The big absence that dialectical critical realism remedies is the absence of absence,[113] or negativity, change, in fact this allows a kind of recursive definition of dialectic as absenting absences of constraints on absenting ills,[114] to further human progress we need to absent ill, or ill

---

113 Absence is not only necessary for being, but change, properly understood, presupposes absence, i.e. the coming into being of new properties or entities and the passing away from being of previously existing ones. Absence yields not only the clue to the vexed problem of dialectic, which may be seen as depending on the rectification of absence (omissions, incompleteness) in a move to greater generality, inclusiveness and coherence, but is necessary for a full understanding of intentional action. For agency is the absenting of absence and this generates an axiology of freedom conceived as depending upon the absenting of constraints and unwanted and unneeded sources of determination. Bhaskar in Bhaskar et al (2010: 15)

114 In ethics, alethic truth is the 'directionality imposed on the education of desire by the reality principle', which will lead 'not to an end state, but to an objective process of universal human self-realisation, eudaimonia or flourishing(-in-nature)' (Bhaskar 2008b: 176). More broadly, he links it with the idea of absenting ills in pursuit of freedom as the truth of, and the good for, human being.

being. And this can be tied up with the non-cognitive generalisation of explanatory critique[115] that we discussed last time. We saw in the cognitive generalisation, or cognitive development of it, that what we were concerned to do, to show, was that if you could explain falsity in a situation or an understanding, and you had a better theory, you could also pass immediately to a negative evaluation of the causes of that causal understanding.

With explanatory critique, we can talk about getting rid of ills and think about the social project as one of improving wellbeing. In fact, what dialectical critical realism does is it looks at various concepts of freedom[116] and shows how they are interconnected with solidarity.

So we start with a very simple concept of agentive freedom, negative and positive freedoms, moving to more complex concepts of emancipation, autonomy, the wellbeing and flourishing.

A simple statement is as follows: 'In the moral realm, alethic truth, the good, is freedom, depending on the absenting of constraints on absenting ills' (Bhaskar 2008b: 212). This in turn ties in with the idea of a dialectical logic immanent in human being to give 'the definition of dialectic as absenting absentive agency, or as the axiology of freedom' (Bhaskar 2008b: 176), and the claim that 'absenting constraints on absenting absences is the alethia of dialectic' (Bhaskar 2008b: 177). Norrie A (2010: 126)

115 [...] the main point is actually to go on from explanatory critique and from cognitive to non-cognitive ills, and these include the non-satisfaction not only of basic physical needs but more generally of what one needs to fulfil one's dharma, one's concretely singularised potentiality – lack of the tools of one's trade, or of free time, of recognition, respect, and so on, and most importantly of course they embrace oppression, including any violation of self determination. Bhaskar in Bhaskar R & Hartwig M(2010: 105)

116 (Ed) For a detailed account of the various concepts of freedom see Forms of Freedom in Norrie A (2010: 141-144)

And the end of the ethical dialectic is a society in which we oriented to the free flourishing of each, as a condition of the free flourishing of all.

Agentive Freedon
The power to start/act a new.

Negative and Postive Freedom
Be free from constraints on/To be free to do.

Emancipation
Universal human emancipation from (unnecessary) constraints.

Autonomy
Possesses the power, knowledge and disposition to act in real interests.

Wellbeing
The absence of ills

Flourishing
The realisation of possibilities.

Eudaimonia
Universal human flourishing.

Table Five: Forms of Freedom

This is to echo a formula that Marx[117] used for his idea of a communist society of the future. We can interpret this more generally as a

---

117 The vision, so nicely articulated by Marx, of a communist society as one in which 'the free development of each is the condition of the free development of all' logically entails that your development and flourishing is as important to me as my own - presupposition so strong that it itself must be universally instantiated in such a society for it to hold at all. This is exactly the same as the idea of the bodhisattva in Mahayana Buddhism, in which the 'no ego' of the realised being

eudaimonistic society, a society oriented to human wellbeing or flourishing. Now this places certain demands on the self at the plane of the stratification of the embodied personality, which are very far reaching indeed, as we will see when we turn to the philosophy of metaReality. Because if the basis of this society is one in which the free development of each is a condition of the free development of all, then this means that your flourishing is as important to me as my own. So it involves the losing of senseless ego that we all, to a greater or lesser extent, possess.

The eudaimonistic society, the goal put forward by dialectical critical realism, depends on the transformation and transcendence of all master/slave-type oppressive relations. Here it is useful to distinguish two concepts of power:[118] power1, which is transformative capacity, and power2, which is oppression. Clearly, what we need to do is for the oppressed to have more of power1 in order to transform the power2 relation between their oppressors and themselves and in order to transform the relationship itself.

Therefore, we have here a combination of a very demanding set of social requirements of social life, and also a very demanding set of requirements of our self, and one, which does not see any incompatibility between those two.

---

engages in the dharmakaya of the whole of humanity, that is, cannot himself be free until each and every being in the cosmos is fully free, in the sense of realised. Bhaskar (2012c: 174)

118 Suppose one distinguishes power1, as the transformative capacity analytic to the concept of agency, from (the transfactual or actual) power2 relations expressed in structures of domination, exploitation, subjugation and control, which I will thematise as generalized master—slave (-type) relation. Bhaskar (2008b: 60)

The other thing perhaps to mention is in the ethical dialectic of dialectical critical realism; a big role is played by what I call the logic of dialectical universalised[119] ability. We can get a gist of this logic by looking at two kinds of ethical dialectics that it postulates. The first, the dialectic of desire or agency: this proceeds from an agent having a desire. Then what is argued is that this desire contains with it a meta-desire to abolish any constraints on that desire. The logic of dialectical universalised ability insists that an agent so committed must be logically committed to the abolition of all dialectically similar constraints. And so it moves in the direction and necessitates a solidarity with others.

Similarly, in the dialectic of discourse the starting point is the expressive veracity of statements of solidarity, which entail commitment to the person and situation one is in solidarity, entailing action, which again, proceeding through the logic of dialectical universalised ability, will be aimed at the transformation of all dialectically similar constraints, and ultimately all dialectical constraints of human freedom and flourishing as such.

---

119 (Ed) I recommend reading Desire and Freedom, Norrie A (2010: 138-139) in which he explores this paragraph and the next in some depth.

Meta-critique of Western Philosophy

DCR generates a very powerful critique of the history of western philosophy. We can see this as being initiated by the polarity between Heraclitus's theories of change, and Parmenides's theories of status. In fact there are two Heraclituses; there is the Heraclitus as interpreted by Plato, and Nietzsche who is a theorist of life and there is the Heraclitus who is a proto transcendental realist[120] who is moving in the direction of theorising explicable change.

The normalisation of ontological monovalance by Plato in his theory of form and analysis of change in terms of difference set up a situation in which western philosophy is dominated by the problem of the one and the many.[121]

---

120 In Bhaskar's account, Heraclitus is a subversive philosopher, as Nietzsche and Deleuze agree, but his subversiveness does not reside in the hypostatisation of becoming in separation from the structuring of being. Heraclitus's radicalism rests rather upon the prototypical meshing of ideas of becoming and the structuring of being, and here Heraclitus foreshadows the critical realist emphasis on the significance of real determinate absence alongside the stratification of reality, the ways in which being and becoming exist in structured relations. For Bhaskar, the denial of absence in favour of the positive sequesters not only the possibility of thinking real absence and change, but also the possibility of thinking the grounds of change, and these are located in underlying structures, relations, mechanisms, and the like. Norrie A (2010: p 212)

121 [...] the problem of 'the one and the other' was central to pre-Socratic philosophy because it essentially concerned the nature of being, what we now call ontology, and how it was possible to understand that many different things might (or might not) possess a single nature such as water, air or some other general substance. The problem of 'the one and the many' in contrast is a problem for Plato and post-Platonic philosophy, for it is the problem of how different things may be grouped together under a scheme of universal categories. There is, it will be noticed, a certain

This is the problem of universal or the problem of induction. What is forgotten is the old problem of the one and the other, which is the problem of change and the essential connection between opposites. But as soon as you situate this problem of the one and the many in the context of actualism then there is no way of avoiding the problems of what I call the transdictive complex,[122] the most familiar of which is the problem of induction. What happens is that the tradition, lacking the concept of structure, has to smuggle in a transcendent realism to complement its empirical realism, or generally anthroporealism,[123] as a new transcendent. This may be Plato's form, Aristotelian nous, or it may be Humean custom, it may be Cartesian certainty, Kantian synthetic

---

parallelism between the terms in which the two problems are described, but the difference is crucial, for the second emerges as the problem of how we know the universal within the particular, and therefore has an essentially epistemological cast in comparison to the ontological cast ('what is the nature of things?') of the one–other problem. Put in different terms, the first problem relates to the nature of change, the second to the nature of difference. Norrie A (2010: 170)

122 The inference from observed to unobserved things. Transdiction has the following forms. Induction is the inference from past to future, transduction is the inference from closed to open systems, retroduction is the inference from actual phenomena to structural causes, and retrodiction is the inference from events to antecedent causes. Retrodiction is the transition in practical explanation from resolved components of a complex to antecedent causes. The ability to retrodict causes presupposes theoretical explanation and retroduction. Retroduction is the transition in theoretical explanation from manifest phenomena to their generating mechanisms. Transduction pertains to the applicability of laws discovered in closed systems to open systems. Irwin L WSCR Glossary (1997)

123 Bhaskar also uses the term "anthroporealism" to refer to the kind of realism (empirical, conceptual, etc.) underpinned by all types of anthropic theory. He argues that every theory necessarily has its own realism (or ontology) behind it: "the question is not whether to be a realist, but what sort of realist to be." Seo M (2014: 74)

apriori, Fichte[124] intellectual intuition, that the new transcendent has to be there in order to underwrite the possibility of universal or general reasoning.

And so there has been a constant tendency or pressure to revert back to the ideas of flux, of incessant change, of ineffable uniqueness until we reach the point where we have the celebration of the Event[125] in philosophers like Badiou[126] when the Event emerges out of the blue unconnected with a pre-existing material context and unconnected with a possibility we have for acting towards it today. So, the co-ordinates offered by DCR, I think, are very powerful ones.

---

124 Johann Gottlieb Fichte (May 1762 – January 1814)

125 An Event is something akin to a rip in the fabric of being, and/or of the social order. It is traumatic for the mainstream, and exhilaratingly transformative for participants. Events are so radical as to even escape Badiou's own ontology. A lot of Badiou's discussions of the Event are negative. An Event is depicted as being other than "being as being", or the normal, mathematically integrated structure of reality. Since there is no general situation or History, something only has 'being' if it belongs to a situation. Events do not belong to situations, events occur outside being-as-being. Robinson A (2014)

126 Alain Badiou (born January 1937)

"Dialectic is the yearning for freedom and the transformative negation of constraints on it." Roy Bhaskar (2008b: 378)

"Reality is a potentially infinite totality, of which we know something but not how much." Roy Bhaskar (2008b: 15)

A Brief Introduction to the Philosophy of metaReality

Gary Hawke[127]

During the last live stream, Roy's health was not good, and there was much going on in his life. It was a testament to his capacity to put others before himself, which drove him to complete the final talk.

However, it is possible that Roy had much more to say on The Philosophy of metaReality (PMR) than he had time. During the final stream, Roy found his rhythm and began to enjoy the process of giving virtual talks. After the stream, we began discussing the next stage. Roy wanted to do a series of follow up sessions, which would form the structure for a deeper look at critical realism and its world applications.

Given the depth of PMR, I would like to offer the reader a short introduction. Within the introduction I will attempt to situate PMR within the general trajectory of critical realism, and also try to address the problem of the spiritual turn (Cravens S 2010) and how best to navigate Bhaskar's use of eastern spiritual philosophical ideas in his philosophy of metaReality.

---

127 A version of this introduction appeared in Polifonia, Cuiabá-MT, v. 23, nº 33, p. 29-36, Jan-Jun., 2016

Throughout this introduction, I would recommend that the reader maintain a connection to two vital ideas within critical realism – The Intransitive dimension and the Transitive dimension. The Intransitive is the dimension where things exist even if we have no knowledge of them. And in critical realism things are not just objects, they can be reasons, or relationships, anything can be a thing so long as it has causal power, so for example within PMR Love is a thing that exits as it has causal power. The Transitive is the dimension in which we have knowledge of things or when the thing has effect on us. For example, "I did not know you loved me until you shared your love for me".

It could also be possible to say that because you have not had an experience of the existence of God, (or as we get deeper into this introduction, the non-dual), does not mean that God does not exits. This argument is made in such critical realism books as *Transcendence: Critical Realism and God* (2004) and *A Fresh Look at Islam in a Multi-Faith World: a philosophy for success through education* (2015). It is the structure of this argument that enables Bhaskar to maintain adherence to the critical realism principle of "seriousness in your philosophy" when he speaks of one of the most important elements of PMR - the non-dual.

It is here in the area of the non-dual that I would like to begin this introduction. *In Reality and Self-Realization: Bhaskar's Metaphilosophical Journey Toward Non-Dual Emancipation.* (2014) Mingyu Seo suggested that we could see the development of CR as a move from dualism to dualistic to non-dual.

Basic or original critical realism (BCR) developed by Bhaskar in his first three books *A Realist Theory of Science, The Possibility of Naturalism, and Scientific Realism and Human Emancipation* is a project of the re-vindication of ontology in both social science and natural science. It attempts this by noticing the split between ontology and epistemology, and how philosophy commits the epistemic fallacy, taking what we know for what is, which makes a philosophy anthropocentric. Dualism here is the mind body problem, the split between facts and values, or society and individual. Dualism is the demi-real, a term used by Bhaskar to indicate that we may feel that something is real, but this is ultimately based on a false belief. If we acknowledge that the world is stratified and within the stratification, there are emergence properties, synchronic emergent properties material (Bhaskar 2015: 97) offers that mind is an emergence property of matter, but cannot be reduce to matter. Applying explanatory critique (Bhaskar 2015: 120) we can see that facts, all things considered, can become values. The transformational model of social activity (Bhaskar 2015: 34) shows that an individual is thrown into a society, but has the power to effect change within that society, so society exits before me, but I can chance society.

With dualism addressed and ontology placed back within philosophy, Bhaskar moves onto the next stage of critical realism that of engaging with the dualistic world or the world of the relative realm. Why is the relative realm the dualistic world, Seo suggests that this can best be answered by seeing the dualistic world as a domain of mediation between the dualism of demi real and non-dual of the metaReal, the dualistic world is the relative real world that we live in.

Within this real we find the constellational aspect that is brought out through the dialectic, yet unlike Hegel's dialectic that aims to create a closed totality of the world, Bhaskar in *Dialectical Critical Realism* (DCR) shows that the world is an open totality subject to change and difference. It is only within a dialectical moment of non-identify can we come to know the world or know the concert universal/singular. We could best describe the structure of DCR through how Bhaskar applies his MELD schema to the relationship of being, the first level (1M) is a level, which thinks or understands being as such and being as non-identity. The second level, (2E), explores being as process, being as involving negativity, change and absence. The third level (3L) explores being as together as internally related and as a whole. The fourth level (4D) understands being as incorporating transformative praxis. (Bhaskar 2012b preface xlix) The dialect then is a deepening process of knowing the stratified constellational nature of being.

If critical realism is a philosophy of science and DCR is a philosophy of dialects, PMR is a philosophy of freedom, love, and creativity; it is a philosophy about you and me, a philosophy that offers identity over difference, unity over split, it is also a philosophy of the non-dual.

Let me stop for a moment and recall a story that Bhaskar use to tell when he talked about PMR, as you move about a busy street how is it that you do not bump into people, even though you may be lost in your thoughts as you walk down the street, you still do not bump into people. What is happening here is a moment of non-duality, you are one with the mass of people, and yet you are an individual. When you watch a movie or read a book, or even as you read this introduction, you are moving beyond yourself, entering into something that is not you, you are removing yourself from yourself, this is the non-dual. When we listen to each other, in the moment of listening this is the non-dual. The non-dual for PMR is not just an eastern spiritual metaphor for being enlightened, it is a real thing, it is an intransitive causal power that when actualised transitively allows both you and I to meet, it allows society to flourish.

In The Philosophy of metaReality: Creativity, love and freedom, Bhaskar describes the non-dual as:

"The basis or ground of the realm of duality, which is non-duality as the non-dual being of ground-state and cosmic envelope."

"The way in which we communicate with other beings, especially human beings, but even more generally, perceive, see, read, follow, understand things in the world; and as a necessary component for any action at all, including speech, thought, etc."

"The deep interior or fine structure of any aspect of being, which through the power of perception, of awareness can be traced back to its ground-state, which provides, as we shall see, a powerful way of disconnecting elements and forms of heteronomy both inside and outside the field of an embodied personality." (Bhaskar 2012b: 2)

There are three things that need to be explored here, as we begin to understand PMR, the cosmic envelope, ground-state, and embodied personality. The cosmic envelope is the space, from which all things manifest, we have encountered a similar idea before in DCR the concrete universal, all thing are interconnected at the cosmic envelope, both you and I are one within the cosmic envelope. When I am at my ground-state or I am at concrete singular, I am in flow, or I have dropped free of my ego, I no longer live in the demi-real, I am, to use a yogachara term, free of my kleshas, unwholesome mind and thoughts.

Free of these egoic contradictions I am then able to engage in the world in right action as an embodied personality at the level of interpersonal relationships, the level of our material transaction, such as work, and social settings, on the level of intrapersonal relationships, and at the level of the natural world. To extend the MELD scheme to included PMR the fifth level, (5A), understand being as reflexive and generally interior. The sixth level, called (6R) understands being as being re enchantment. The seventh level (7Z) understands being as incorporating the primacy of identity over difference and unity over split and in particular understands being as non-duality.

In the closing paragraph of Dialectics: The Pulse of Freedom (2008b) Bhaskar writes:

"Alethic truth, as optimally grounding reason, can be the rational cause of transformative negating agency in absenting constraints on self-emancipation, that is, on the liberation of our causal powers to flourish. For to exist is to be able to become, which is to possess the capacity for self-development, a capacity that can be fully realized only in a society founded on the principle of universal concretely singularized human autonomy in nature. This process is dialectic; and it is the pulse of freedom."

This idea of the pulse of freedom is taken up and becomes the manifesto of PMR:

"The philosophy of metaReality describes the way in which this very world nevertheless depends upon, that is, is ultimately sustained by and exists only in virtue of the free, loving, creative, intelligent energy and activity of non-dual states of our being and phases of our activity. In becoming aware of this we begin the

process of transforming and overthrowing the totality of structures of oppression, alienation, mystification and misery we have produced; and the vision opens up of a balanced world and of a society in which the free development and flourishing of each unique human being is understood to be the condition, as it is also the consequence, of the free development and flourishing of all." (Bhaskar 2012b: vii)

Having set out the aims of the Philosophy of metaReality, explored the use of the non-dual, and shown how PMR links back to BCR and DCR it becomes possible to see how the 17 basic principles of PMR are sublations of Bhaskar's early works.

1. The Principle of the Inexorability of Ontology (irreducibility of being)

2. The Principle of the All-inclusiveness of Ontology

3. The Principle of Dispositional Realism

4. The Principle of Categorical Realism

5. The Principle of Alethic Realism

6. The Principle of the TINA Formation

7. The Definition of Liberation as Shedding

8. The Understanding of Liberation as Dependent on Asymmetry

9. The Theory of the Ground-state

10. The Theory of the Cosmic Envelope

11. The Theory of Transcendence

12 The Principle of Transcendental Identification in My Consciousness

13. The Principle of Co-presence

14. The Principle of the Primacy of Self-Referentiality

15. The Principle of Re-enchanting Reality

16. The Principle of an Unlimited or Unbounded Self

17. The Principle of MetaReality

The first seven principles have been encountered before through basic and dialectical critical realism. And within this introduction, I would like take time to explore just one principle, which I also think will be beneficial to the reader, when thinking about how one might apply PMR, and will expose an overview of the other principles.

Principle 11 the theory of transcendence states there are four ways in which we can experience transcendence or the non-dual.

Transcendence into or Transcendental Retreat or Clearing, this is a sense, in which we step back from objectivity and notice our own subjective experience, a great gestalt exercise here is to ask, what do I see, what do I notice, what do I feel, what do I know, what do I not know. In keeping with the first Moment and second Edge of MELD this is non-identify, and absence, we do not just accept the object or thing we step back notice the gap between observer and observed and within the gap ask what is there.

Transcendence into or Transcendental Identification in consciousness, as we move fully into the object or thing, noticing our connection, we become part of a new level or totality of connectedness, which relates to the 3L of MELD, this can be simply experience when we look at a flower, a sunset, or a beautiful painting, there is no longer a gap.

Transcendence On or Transcendental Agency, this is when we are completely active within the act, it is both being mindful and mindless, our agency is focused, it is alive, and it is free. I began writing this introduction at 8 am it is now 6 pm, and throughout that time, I have focused completely on the creative act of writing, not aware of the passing of time.

Transcendence With or Transcendental Teamwork, this is the moment when you and I work mindfully, when there appears to be one mind at work, such as when playing sports, it is the group unity in the moment. Both Transcendental teamwork and Agency are the transformative praxis of 4D within MELD.

For me the principle 11 is at the heart of PMR, for without transcendence there can be no love, and without love there can be no creativity, and without creative there is no drive for freedom, and without a drive for freedom, we will never break the blocks that occlude our emancipation.

The philosophy of metaReality is a philosophy of emancipation; it calls us out to be more that we are. It demands that we do the work of freeing not just ourselves but all sentient beings, it has a profound ecology, we are both of the world and in the world, and as such, we need to protect the world. It is a philosophy allowing for difference as an aspect of identity. It makes room for both western and eastern philosophy, and it extends Bhaskar's project of maintaining the importance of the intransitive and transitive. It paves the way for the next step in critical realism, interdisciplinary, and Bhaskar's move into education, disability studies, wellbeing, ecology, and conflict management.

The philosophy of metaReality, is a philosophy of theory-practice consistency, it offers a view of the world in which we are at the deepest and finest level connected, it suggests that this deep ontological level, can be known if we are prepared to undertake the practice of letting go of the personal and social blocks that occlude our freedom. It is a radical departure from what went before within critical realism, but when viewed within the stream of the development of critical realism, from dualism to duality to non-dual, it is possible to retroduct metaReality thinking within Bhaskar's early stages of critical realism.

I would go as far to say that the philosophy of metaReality under-labours for original critical realism and dialectical critical realism. At the beginning of critical realism Bhaskar asked what must the world be like for science to exists, with metaReality Bhaskar now asks what must the world be like for you and I to live free.

Moreover, it is a philosophy of love.

"Love in fact may be thought of as being a basic or defining characteristic of transcendental identification or union as such, a binding characteristic at the level of the cosmic envelope, and a cohering or binding force in social life". (Bhaskar 2012b: 7)

"It is not that there are the starry heavens above and the moral law within, as Kant would have it; rather, the true basis of your virtuous existence is the fact that the starry heavens are within you, and you are within them." Roy Bhaskar (2012b: 350)

Chapter Three

Non-Dualism

The Philosophy of

MetaReality

Live Stream took place 2nd June 2014

"The philosophy of metaReality brings to the fore non-duality as the ground, mode of constitution and deep structure of the world of duality and dualism." Roy Bhaskar (2012b: 314)

"The necessity for transcendence as constitutive of creativity and emergence in science, the arts, education, practical life, etc. shows the creator or innovator to be a kind of practical mystic. Moreover I want to insist that there is a sense in which every genuinely human act, as actually or potentially transformative of the world (and necessarily as transformative, in the sense that without that act the state of affairs which ensued would have been otherwise), involves creativity, i.e. the production of something new, the production of something that would not have occurred without that act." Roy Bhaskar (2012b: 129)

Introduction and More Levels of Ontology

Basic Critical Realism consists of transcendental realism, critical naturalism and a theory of explanatory critique, philosophy of science, philosophy of social science and an intervention in ethics. Dialectical critical realism also includes the first venture into the topic of spiritualty, which I explained in my book *From East to West*[128] when I called the resulting system Transcendental Dialectical Critical Realism. [129] The Philosophy of metaReality is a further development that it presupposes the previous developments.

Now you will recall from last time that dialectical critical realism is a four-level system, properly known as MELD, in which we understand being as non–identity, being as structure, being as difference. Which is at

---

128 Bhaskar (2015) second edition From East To West: Odyssey of a Soul, Routledge, London

The essential thesis of this book is that man is essentially God (and therefore also essentially one, but also essentially unique); and that, as such, he is essentially free and already en-lightened, a freedom and enlightenment which is overlain by extraneous, heteronomous determinations which both (a) occlude and (b) qualify this essential fact. To reclaim and realise his essential freedom, man has to shed both the illusion that he is not essentially Godlike and free and the constraining heteronomous determinations (constituting an objective world of illusion, duality and alienation) which that illusion grounds. To become free or realise his freedom man must thus shed both the illusions that he is not (essentially) and that he is (already, only and completely) free! Bhaskar (2015: ix)

129 I believe that we have got to think through all the categorical domains of dialectical critical realism and that this transcendental deepening or radicalisation of dialectical critical realism (which I am calling transcendental dialectical critical realism) will lead us to see that really the best action, and indeed most action, is basic, that is, pretty spontaneous; it is not calculating instrumental action. Bhaskar (2012a: 135)

the very beginning of critical realism we had began with a double argument around ontology. It was an argument for ontology against its reduction to epistemology, which resulted in a critique of what they call the epistemic fallacy and the differentiation of the intransitive dimension of science and knowledge from the transitive dimension.

That was one part of the argument, the other part of the argument was the argument for a new ontology because I maintained that the attempt to do without ontology in philosophy had been fraudulent and actually masked the generation of an implicit ontology which was a Humean empiricist one in which the world was conceived as flat, undifferentiated and unchanging.

And in place of that ontology, I argued for an ontology of structure and difference. The pre-concept of basic critical realism in a way was non-identity critically, that being was something else, it was not the same as knowledge, that structures and generative mechanisms, causal laws, were not the same as empirical regularities. So this was the main characteristic of the first level of ontology: non-identity, structure, and difference, resulting in a critique of what was called actualism, which was the reduction of the real to the actual and thence to the empirical.

The second level of ontology, which was broached in dialectical critical realism, took the giant step of thematising negativity, absence and change. I argued the world was not unchanging and change was irreducible to being. This took the form of a critique of the doctrine of ontological monovalence and the generation of an analysis of change and negativity in terms of the key concept of absence.

The third level thematised relations between things as internal as well as extensional and took things together as a whole. So we have at this third level of being, an understanding of being, concepts of holistic causality, totality, the concrete universal, constellationality, and many other interesting concepts.

Then at the fourth level of understanding being we understand it as incorporating human agency, and transformative praxis. This is the level that had already been broached in the philosophy of social science, critical naturalism.

Now the Philosophy of metaReality developed our understanding of three other categorical levels. The fifth level thematises being as interior, as reflexive, and being as, in a certain sense, spiritual and the fifth sense is something we talk about as 5A, the fifth aspect. Then the sixth level is the level or 6R, the sixth realm, in which we understand being as re-enchanted, we understand meanings and values as real and not just subjective impositions of human beings, so that the world contains value, whether humans beings are here or not to recognise it. The seventh level, 7Z which completes the system, understands being in terms of the primacy of the identity over difference, and the primacy of unity over split.

And these three levels are the levels thematised by the philosophy of metaReality.[130]

---

130 The A in 5A stands for aarh! in the moment of transcending, of creative inspiration or eureka; of bliss, joy, release and relief. The R in 6R stands for resonance, ripple or ray (the result of esoteric or exoteric reciprocity). Thus R as re-enchantment reinforces 1M more, 3L love; it also indicates

1M	Non-Identity
2E	Absence
3L	Totality
4D	Transformative Praxis
5A	Reflextive
6R	Re-Enchanted
7Z	Primacy of Identity

Table Six: PMR thematised as MELD(ARZ)

Now, the seventh level is very interesting because in a way what it does is it reverses the standpoint of the first level (1M). At the first level we stress the non-identity between things and categories. The concept that comes very much to the fore is difference. The seventh level we assert the primacy of identity, after all over difference. One paradigm of this might be two people in conversation, totally absorbed in what the other is saying. So that when you are talking and totally focused and listening to you, and then our consciousnesses are in transcendental identification although our bodies and our beings remain distinct. So in what we characterise as the world of duality, the world of subject and object, our consciousnesses are united.

'really!?', as in a surprise, the edginess implicit in dare do, consummated in the 'aarh' of transcendence, raised and stabilised in awakening. So that the A in ZA is a resonating response or echo, a reaffirmation or reprise of the 5A of 'aarh', the aha! Bhaskar (2012b: 285)

Now this sense in which we are positioned between subject and object is transcended at the level of philosophy and metaReality does not involve the transcendence of or the abolition of the physical world of duality; that still remains. Secondly, we have to understand the sense in which we talk about the primacy of identity. The sense of identity here is very different from the punctiform atomistic identities critiqued in transcendental realism. The sense of identity here is like the identity one has, one might feel, with a symphony or with a beautiful picture or with a sunset. It is a differentiated developing identity, a moving identity. Still, some arguments would have to be given for asserting anything like the primacy of identity over difference in the sort of world in which we live.

Let me start with some low-level arguments from our ordinary uses of concepts: so if I say that I and Donald[131] are of different heights then this presupposes that we have something in common, namely height. If we move from the primacy of identity over difference to the primacy of unity over split, you might want to think about how we would accommodate understanding of the different universe other than by incorporating its incorporation effectively into our universe, or our universe's incorporation into its universe so that we would be dealing with a mega universe. It seems difficult to theorise, to understand something outside the universe when we come into contact with it. It would always be in our universe in some sense.

I want to look at a stronger sort of argument from the history of philosophy in a moment. But let me differentiate three characteristic

---

131 (Ed) During the live broadcast Donald Clark was running the backroom ensuring that everything went smoothly with the broadcast.

philosophies: both critical realism as it has been established up to the Philosophy of metaReality, which I think is the best possible way of understanding what happens in the world of duality.

Then there is the Philosophy of metaReality, which argues there is a world of non-duality,[132] of the transcendence of those dualities sustaining the world of duality and there is the third type of philosophy corresponding to a third kind of world, which we call demi-reality. This is the world of duality in which the differences between things are sharpened into antagonistic contradictions and horrendous splits. One could certainly argue that we live in a world of duality, which is dominated by demi-reality in which oppressive structures hold sway.[133]

The argument of metaReality would be that these structures could not hold sway, without being passively pre-supposed by a deeper level, which is in fact a level of non-duality. Once we recognise this level, this gives us an indication of an alternative force of power in being.

---

132 We can contrast nondualism as a philosophy with nondual awareness as an experience (with the caveat that, technically, according to some, nondual experience is not an experience proper). While nondualism is a philosophical construct that uses words in an attempt to describe what is ultimately real, nondual awareness is an experience in which the subject-object dualities that characterize human experience appear to vanish. This "collapse" of the subject-object duality can be whole or partial, and last for varying lengths of time. Taft. M. W. (2014:2)

133 I shall define the first evolution from CR to DCR as the "transformation from dualism to duality." The "transformation from duality to constellational identification" signifies the second evolution from DCR to metaReality. Bhaskar uses the term "dualism" to represent the realm of the "irreal" or "demireal. Seo M (2014: 3)

The metaReal
Nonduality
Groundstate, Love,
Transcendental Self

The Relative Real
Duality
The Embodied Personality
The Dialectic of the Pulse of Freedom

The Demi-real
Dualism
The Egoic self, Split,
Alienation, Ideology

Figure Nine: Levels of the Real

Hegel and The Life and Death Struggle[134]

Let us look at the philosopher who was trying to head in a similar direction, not the same direction but a similar direction, Hegel, and I am going to talk about a passage in Hegel from arguably his greatest work, *Phenomenology of Mind*, quite a famous passage, which is known as the life and death struggle.[135]

Hegel asked us to imagine two primitive beings, let us call them savages, who are engaged in a fight to the death, and as one gains victory over the other and stands over the other Hegel asks the question, Why does the winner spare the life of the one who loses? Hegel's answer is that he spares the life of the loser in order that the loser can praise the winner, can say how marvellous he was, can act as a witness to his bravery

---

134 The relation of both self–consciousnesses is in this way so constituted that they prove themselves and each other through a life–and–death struggle. They must enter into this struggle, for they must bring their certainty of themselves, the certainty of being for themselves, to the level of objective truth, and make this a fact both in the case of the other and in their own case as well. And it is solely by risking life that freedom is obtained; only thus is it tried and proved that the essential nature of self–consciousness is not bare existence, is not the merely immediate form in which it at first makes its appearance, is not its mere absorption in the expanse of life. Hegal GWF (Author), Bailey J.B (Translator) (2003: 107), The Phenomenology of Mind, Dover Philosophical Classics. Also see Bhaskar (2008b: 4.5) Master and Slave: From Dialectics of Reconciliation to Dialectics of Liberation

135 I particularly like G. W. F. Hegel's life–and–death struggle here, because this shows why mutual death or destruction is not the only alternative to our current crisis. As you will recall, the life-and-death struggle is when you have two savages or primeval human beings fighting to the finish. They are both prepared to lose their life in order to win, and then a point of victory comes to one and the question is: why doesn't he kill the other? Hegel says he doesn't kill him because he prefers to have the other bearing witness to his strength, to his bravery. Bhaskar R in Hartwig, M & Morgan J (2013: 209)

and valour and courage and struggle, and, in short, in order that the winner's victory and the power of that may be possible are recognised. This starts a long tradition in the history of philosophy, which takes as its theme the struggle for recognition.

An alternative interpretation of the life and death struggle, which comes from the materialist direction of Engle and Marx, they say, that is rubbish, the reason why the winner spares the life of the person he vanquishes is in order to make the person a slave, in order to make him a servant and do labour for him.

This itself sets up an alternative dialectic of interpretation because then we have the whole question of what happens to the slave? Well, the slave, in acting for the lazy master, develops his or her powers and eventually it reaches a point when the slave can overthrow the master and, even more importantly, overthrow the master/slave relationship. So that develops in the history of the Left as a struggle for emancipation and we have these two themes a struggle for recognition, the struggle to transcend master/slave by oppression as powerful themes and it is still very much present in contemporary political philosophy.

What Hegel is doing in his analysis, the Left are doing in their analysis, is presuming that there are arguments why a unity of the sort should be sustained.

The Argument for metaReality

I want to now develop the argument for the Philosophy of MetaReality more formally and my argument is that there are three senses in which identity is prior to, more important than, more important ontologically than, difference, and unity more important than alienation or split. The first sense is a sense in which identity or non-duality is necessary for the constitution of social life, necessary for its reproduction or transformation.

Therefore, we have identity as a mode of constitution. The second sense is one in which identity is the basis of social life and the third sense is one in which identity and non-duality is a deep interior of social being and indeed of being itself. First looking at the arguments as to why identity is important in the constitution of social life I want to differentiate four forms of transcendence of duality.

Transcendental
Identification in
Consciousness

Transcendental
Agency

Transcendental
Holism

Transcendental
Self

Table Seven: Four Forms of The Transcendent

121

What is *Transcendental[136] Identification in Consciousness*? This is what happens when you are reading a book or looking at the television and you are completely absorbed in the book or on the television and someone comes into the room, says something and you lose your place in the book, or you lose the developing plot and you need to ask someone else what happened. Or you go back and you read the paragraph you were on, a pacifist philosophy book, and resume the thread of the argument. So, metaReality argues that a transcendental identification in consciousness is necessary for any social interaction or any perception to take place. You might think this is absurd and you might be listening to me talking now and you say:

"Well, I'm not in identity with your consciousness, I'm not in identity with your words, I don't agree with them to the extent that I can understand them, and that's I can't really understand them and so how can you talk about transcendental identification in consciousness by saying I can't understand what you're saying?"

I will say, yes, but you were in identification with the words or the sounds that I made in order to say, to come and tell me, that you do not understand them, you have to be in identification with them, you have to be able to say what they are. And so, really, transcendental identification in consciousness of the thought that you have when you are reading a newspaper or looking at television is a very simple and common thing. It is logically the same sort of thing that has been traditionally theorised under the topic of non-duality in religious contexts, the idea of

136 (Ed) In Original and Dialectical Critical Realism the transcendental was the art of asking what must the world be like or what kind of things exist. In PMR the transcendental is the art of going beyond or going beyond being.

much meditation is to reach a point where there are not two things but just one thing and that is the transcendental consciousness that you are aiming for, whether it is eastern-type mediation or western-type prayer. This paradigm has always seemed a very difficult one, probably because the object that you are being enjoined to become one with is difficult, not because the procedure itself is.

There are many jokes that could be told there about this kind of state of non-duality, thus it is critical for someone leading a meditation group, after he has got the people in the group meditating and supposedly in the state of non-duality, to ask them who is in a state of transcendental consciousness? Put up your hands, he will say. So, of course, say, 40 or 50 per cent put up their hands and he will immediately dismiss them because the fact that they responded in that way showed they were not in a state of non-duality, they were split between what he was saying and what they were supposed to be doing.

Another incident that can illustrate the traditional context of this, Archbishop Carey, the Archbishop of Canterbury, was asked by a journalist how long he spent praying. He replied on a typical day, about 40-50 seconds if I am lucky and it scandalised the journalist and his audience because they assumed the Archbishop must be praying for five or six hours a day. Of course, he was trying to pray for five or six hours, trying to get in that state of non-dual consciousness and only obtaining it for a very short moment of time. It becomes less mysterious this idea of non-duality when we see how routinely we must achieve it in an everyday context.

Let me move on from transcendental identification in consciousness to the idea of *Transcendental Agency*. This is the idea that in any action there must be a point when the thought of your action, the thought of what you are doing, is no longer a distinct thing from your doing it. In fact all you have is your doing it. So, for example, I can think about how I am going to cook dinner tonight but at some point I have to actually do it. I could think about what sentence I am going to say next, at some point I just have to do it, and then when I do it there is no longer the thought and the viewing as distinct entities, there is just the doing. And those kind of spontaneous acts, non-dual acts, are called by philosophers basic acts,[137] and they have been thematised in western analytical philosophy in that sort of way. So, again, they are not so completely new to philosophical consciousness. But the theme that unites them with transcendental identification in consciousness, mainly the transcendence of duality, has not being brought out.

The third kind of thing, from a transcendence that we are routinely familiar with, is *Transcendental Holism*. Transcendental holism occurs when you are listening to a group or an orchestra and they are playing in complete harmony, complete unity, with each other.

Supposing I often cook dinners with Rebecca, then she may have certain things that she customarily does and I may have things which I

---

137 Basic acts are a logical precondition for other forms of action, unmediated by any prior thought, or immediate – things that we just do, spontaneously – which PMR (Philosophy of metaReality) links to the non-dual meta-Real in the concept of SPONTANEOUS RIGHT-ACTION. Hartwig M Ed (2007) Agency, Dictionary of Critical Realism Routledge

customarily do and we will appear to be cooking the dinner, that is are cooking a dinner, as one.

You will know today that the World Cup is happening in Brazil,[138] so you have probably, if you are at all interested, seen examples of players effortlessly anticipating other players and balls being passed superbly from one part of the field to another and the passing resulting in a goal or a tremendous save, examples of transcendental holism. There are other kinds of examples, which may be of interest to social science.

For example, how come that in a crowded street when there are so many people on the pavement there are so few accidents, that we do not bump into each other? How come so seldom when we are having a telephone conversation do we talk over each other. How does turn taking happen? These are all examples of transcendental holism.

The fourth kind of the transcendental is the *Transcendental Self*, which takes me, for the purposes of this presentation, into the second sense in which identity is prior to difference in social life.

It takes me to the theory of the self.

---

138 (Ed) In 2014 when Donald and I first began to discuss working with Roy on the streamed talks that the text is based on, we had to ensure that the dates of the live recordings did not clash with the 2014 FIFA World Cup being held in Brazil. Roy was a keen Football fan and well known for being a supporter of Manchester United football club.

The Theory of The Self

I would start by saying that we all have three ideas of the self: there is the idea of self as an ego. That is as something distinct and separate from everything else in the world. And that idea of self as an ego is, I think, a total illusion. It is false, but it is nevertheless the idea that is at the heart of capitalism and capitalistic societies. Then there is the sense of the self as an embodied personality.[139] Now this sense of the self is real, you are an embodied personality; in a way which are not separate from everyone else. But the problem with it is that what counts as your self varies from context to context. Do you count your pets as part of yourself, or your husband, or your wife? If you are a male, is your car, if you have one, a part of your self? Probably it is.

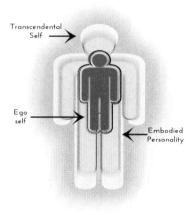

Figure Ten: The Theory of The Self

---

139 [...] embodied personality (itself tripartite in structure being constituted at the very least by mind, emotional makeup and physical embodiment) and a transcendentally real ground-state. Bhaskar (2012b: lx)

Then of course the self is very variable because we grow older, we learn more, we forget some things and get taller and then shorter through the life cycle. In short, we are dealing with a very relative and a contextually shifting sense of the self.

There is a third sense of the self, which is a sense of the self that I call our ground state. This is our transcendentally real self and one can begin to get a grasp of this sense of the self when you have someone like Hume or Nietzche coming into our room and saying well, you know I have searched everywhere for myself and I can assure you that no self exists. Then you turn round to them and say, who is telling me this? Who is it who is telling me this? This is the transcendental self, which they are pre-supposing in the very act of denying it. Of course, that is a logically sound point but can one give a sort of more intuitive sense of how you have and can contact this sense.

It is characteristic perhaps of the post-modern predicament that the idea of a fractured self, that we are split, that when it comes to trying to decide what we want or do we find there are five or six or seven voices in our head. So people often say to me, well, which is the transcendental self of those six or seven voices that I am hearing? I say to them the transcendental self is the listener, ok there are six or seven voices you are hearing but there is only one listener and that is you.

And when you get a grip on the idea of the listener, then you have a grip on the idea of an agency which can restore, or begin a process of working towards a restoring, a robust, unitary, integrated self, a self which is not fractured.

More intuitively even, perhaps, you could say that your ground state is you on a good day. It is when the sun is shining, you are being perfectly charming and generous to everyone and the world is smiling back at you and confirming you - you on an exceptional day. Or we can think of it being your higher self, what you would do when you were in your higher self and we have this sense of it being something you can be in or not in.

When you are not in your higher self, when you are not in your ground state, of course your ground state is still there, and you are still in it but you are also in a lot of other things. You are in your sense of ego or you are in aspects of your embodied personality, you know, your greed or vanity or jealousy, which is interfering with your ground state.

So this is the sense in which metaReality posits a sense of identity, which is a basis for everything else in the social world, our ground state.[140] In the metaphysics that is developed there we have the picture of everyone having ground states, like everything having a ground state, of you being happy in ground state and with ground states with all things lying on or being connected by what I call the cosmic envelope.

---

140 Now turning to the first modality of non-duality. The ground-state itself is of course a being's transcendentally real self. Thus we have the concept of the transcendental self. Then, to simplify things, let us take the case of the human being's transcendentally real self—at the level of the ground-state or cosmic envelope we have the consciousness of the transcendentally real self. This is a supramental level of consciousness, which we may call transcendental consciousness. This is consciousness at or of the ground-state. This is the consciousness which monitors conscious activity and is in principle distinct from the consciousness of the embodied personality, and witnesses or watches or is aware of the total holistic field of the agent's activity Bhaskar (2012b: 6)

We can take a passage from Rumi, the great poet, which expresses this. He says:

"Every forest branch moves differently in the breeze, But as they sway they connect at the roots."[141]

They, as we do, are connected at the ground states.

The third sense in which identity is prior to, or more important than, difference in social life relates to the deep interior of social being. It relates to the deep interior of all being and this is the sense in which mystics have maintained that if you go deeply enough into anything, in that thing you will find something wonderful, pure bliss, in Hindu traditions, Sat-Chit-Anand, [142] in the Christian tradition perhaps a wonderful sense of unconditional love.

In Buddhists tradition, you might describe this as emptiness, Sunyata[143]. Or you might describe it a Buddha nature, so you have Buddhists monks meditating on things like dishcloths, stools, rats, and finding in them, in their deep interior, finding in them the Buddha

---

141 Taken as a metaphor for the cosmos this, along with much else in the philosophy of meta-Reality, is very much in keeping with deep ecology. Most of the main meta-Reality concepts are at least implicitly present in deep ecology, including anti-anthropism and a concept of the intrinsic value of being, and an emphasis on self-realisation as a cumulative process, a conception that like yours is significantly indebted to East. Bhaskar in Bhaskar R & Hartwig M (2010: 192)

142 (Ed) Reality, seen through the discovery of Brahman as sat or ultimate being, cit or pure consciousness, and ananda or perfect bliss.

143 (Ed) Sunyata, in Buddhist philosophy, the voidness that constitutes ultimate reality; Sunyata is seen not as a negation of existence but rather as the undifferentiation out of which all apparent entities, distinctions, and dualities arise.

nature. This sense of the deep interior of things is of course something that we can invoke and have seen invoked.

For example, when Ghandi was leading the struggle for Indian independence against the British and row after row of Indians were being mowed down by the callous hitting of British troops, he was conjoining them to see to the deep interior of these beings, to see that they were also, deep down, sources of love and creativity like oneself, and not just their surface form.

Therefore, this third sense is a sense, which really has to be experienced rather than a sense, which can be demonstrated by transcendental philosophical argumentation.

The view of the world metaReality gives is one in which beings in their ground states are connected by the cosmic envelope[144] at a very deep level of analysis, and sustain a more superficial world of non-duality in which differences arise. And in this world of duality, in particular historical epochs or particular situations and contexts, categorical error, such as is exemplified by the ego, the idea that you can be separate and distinct from every other person, hold sway.

---

144 Transcendental identification in consciousness and transcendental agency are necessary features of human life. It is not difficult to see that we can transcendentally identify with anything, and this means since our transcendental identification is an equating in consciousness, that the whole of the universe must be implicitly conscious too. (This depends upon dispositional realism.) Thus we are bound together in one cosmic envelope. Bhaskar (2012b: 339)

Reciprocity
Transcendental Identification in Consciousness
Co-Presence

Table Eight: Mechanisms of Identification

MetaReality posits three main mechanisms of identification, of making oneself one with another or something else in the world of duality. The first is *Reciprocity*, so if I smile at you then you smile back at me. The second is *Transcendental Identification in Consciousness*, when I am totally absorbed in what you are saying or vice versa. The third is the most radical. Called *Co-presence,*[145] that is when I come to see that you are actually not distinct from me, you are not really something, which I have reciprocal relations with, not something, which I can identify with transcendentally but actually are a part of me, that you are in me, and this is called co-presence. It provides very strong arguments of not harming

---

145 This means that just as consciousness was implicitly enfolded in all being, all beings are implicitly enfolded within my consciousness and therefore within my being. This is a truly extraordinary result. It will be remembered that the western philosopher Kant was inspired by two things above all: *'the starry heavens above me' and 'the moral law within me'*. The theory of co-presence says yes the starry heavens are above me, but they are also within me, enfolded within me, like everything else in the universe. I contain the totality. But on this theory externality does not collapse. For just as the whole world is enfolded within me, I am enfolded within the whole world, more particularly within every object in the world. Bhaskar (2012b: 71)

or hurting the other, because in hurting the other you are actually hurting or harming a part of yourself. At the same time, if you want to be free then you want all to be free because all are co-present within you.

The philosophy of metaReality has some very radical implications, which extend the dialectic of freedom in dialectical critical realism. Because if you have elements in your embodied personality which are inconsistent with your ground state, then your intentionality will be split. If you have an ego, which is there, or if you have jealousy or prejudices, which are there, which are inconsistent with your ground state then you will not be able to achieve your objectives in life. According to this way of looking at things there is not anything you can achieve other than self-realisation, which means coming into unity with your ground state. And that is the only thing that you can feasibly, the only objective you can feasibly have in life and that provides a sort of ideal of negative freedom.[146]

When you are in your ground state you can realise your objectives, or some of them, without inconsistency, your intentionality is not split. However, you may have objectives, and your ground state will certainly have objectives, being co-present with all the other ground states, to end poverty in the world and then of course you cannot just do it by working on yourself.

What you will have to do is you will have to work on all four planes of social being that now you will be working as a negatively free,

---

146 The second form is Isaiah Berlin's negative freedoms (lack of constraints), which are tantamount to positive enabling freedoms to act. Alderson P (2013: 241)

most efficient agent of transformative change to produce the state of eudaimonia,[147] which was the goal of dialectical critical realism. Let us remember some of the ways we characterise this goal. Well one of the ways was in terms of the sublime formula, that eudaimonistic society is one in which the free development, the free flourishing of each, is a condition of the free flourishing of all.

And what this means is that Rebecca's flourishing, or Donald's free flourishing, is as important to me as my own and what that involves is not having an ego, that involves not having a sense of my interest separate and different from Donald's.

Of course, we are so far removed from this goal, most of us, and in most of our living moments, that that is the goal that Marx formulated in his vision of a communist society, and that is the goal that Mahayana Buddhists formulate as the goal, [148] which is necessary for true enlightenment. It is not just your own realisation; it has to be the realisation of all.

---

147 To be fully in your dharma you would need to live in a society that accepted the principle of everyone being in their dharma everywhere. If you had such a society it would be a eudaimonistic society, a society in which the free development of each is a condition of the free development of all. Bhaskar in Bhaskar R & Hartwig, M (2010: 20)

148(Ed) The Bodhisattva vow is taken by Mahayana Buddhists to attain complete enlightenment for the sake of all sentient beings. One who has taken the vow is nominally known as a Bodhisattva.

Figure Eleven: The Embodied Personality Split from The Ground State

Before I end this section, I want to comment on, something about the ground state qualities so you have a sense of them. What are the properties of the ground state? We know that the ego or jealousy or prejudices are not them, but what are they then? Well, corresponding to the MELD scheme of 1M to 4D we have characteristically different kinds of qualities. At 1M it is *Will, Consciousness, Energy*; at 2E it is *Creativity* and everything that arises from and is associated. At 3L it is *Love*; at 4D it is *Spontaneous Right Action*. Then at 5A, just to extend it a bit, it would be seeing your intentionality reflected in world, this would be successful *Reflected Praxis*. So this will give you sense of the qualities of the ground state.

1M   Will, Consciousness, Energy

2E   Creativity

3L   Love

4D   Right Action

5A   Reflextive Praxis

Table Nine: MELD as Qualities of The Ground State

The Prism of metaReality

Then the last topic I want to look at before we break for a few minutes is the extension to social ontology that the identification of this realm makes possible. When you look at the world through the prism of metaReality and allow yourself to identify and recognise non-dual states, then you see that commercial transactions of any sort presuppose a deeper level of trust and solidarity.

If I go up to a newsagent, and ask him for a copy of The Guardian and I do not make any effort to go to a wallet or a pocket, then he may be suspicious that I am not going to pay him for The Guardian and refrain from making to hand over a newspaper to me. In fact, that little parable is the form of all commercial transactions, all commercial transactions that presuppose something like, in fact, the development of the golden rule: Do unto others as you would be done by.[149]

In fact, the way they presuppose it really, in most cases, involve a development of it towards being called the platinum rule,[150] because you are not trying to do unto the newsagent what I would be done by but do

---

149 (Ed) The Golden Rule or law of reciprocity is the principle of treating others as one would wish to be treated oneself. It is a maxim of altruism seen in many human religions, human cultures, and animal kingdoms.

150 Interpreted not as an abstract universal, but as 'presupposing dialectical universality and concrete singularity': do unto others, not as you would do unto yourself, but as you would do unto them if you were they, not you". Bhaskar (2012b 344-5) I am grateful to Stephen Shashoua of the Three Faiths Forum, London, for calling my attention to the fact that this rule is known in interfaith and other circles as the Platinum Rule. Hartwig M, Why I'm a critical realist (note 28) in Ed Bhaskar, R, Esbjörn-Hargens, S, Hedlund, N, Hartwig, M, (2016)

unto him what he would be done by, and more especially what is ground state, I would argue, would be done by. Perhaps you should not introduce the ground state there for just routine commercial transactions as embodied personality, but as an ethical ideal we would have the ground state there. So then, disposition of social life as at the world of duality is actually sustained by a substratum, a metaReal substratum.

Let me give you some other glimpses of it, which it will be obvious to you when I say them, the world of commercial transactions again sustained by domestic labour. In the realm of domestic labour, we do not have instrumental action with our children, we do not have a contract or exchange relations but we have, or what we try and have, is unconditional love.[151]

Then again if you look at social activity such as war through the prism of metaReality you begin to see that war could not happen without a whole lot of peace going. The combat between the soldiers at the front, presupposes peaceful activities of getting supplies to the soldiers, the mobilisation of the consciousness around the idea of war, and the loving support of their sisters and wives at home, a whole lot of peace of things that have to happen for war to be possible.

---

151 In the philosophy of metaReality love plays a crucial role. 'Love', in Bhaskar's terminology, 'is the totalising, unifying, healing force in the universe. And, just by virtue of there being a "universe" (one-verse), it is the most powerful force in being" (Bhaskar 2012b: 175). Hence, the central place of love is intrinsically connected to the fundamental role of non-duality/unity/identity in Bhaskar's general ontology. [...] Human love is thus by no means confined to love for another human being, but beginning with self-love, it radiates in ever-widening circles to encompass all human beings, all beings and finally the cosmic envelope, the sphere in which the ground-states of all beings are interrelated. Gunnarsson, L (2014:119)

MetaReality is deepening our reality in social ontology because we do not normally notice these things and creative philosophy here is acting as an underlabourer and identifying the sources that can be used to produce a better world, eventually. Because there is a huge asymmetry here: if we take a couple formed by peace and war, we can have a society without war, a society with all peace.

But we cannot, I would argue, have a society, which is all war, that is war without peace. So there is an ontological argument that the metaReal level is deeper, and sustains, and is a necessary condition for the level that we normally notice.

In the next session, we look at some of the applications, some of the implications, of the Philosophy of metaReality.

The Application of The Philosophy of MetaReality

I now want to talk about some of the implications and applications of metaReality. I will start by talking about two big topics: modernity and comparative religion and spirituality, but then I will go on to more everyday topics including conflict resolution and learning.

When I wrote the metaReality books[152] I was doing a lot of work in India[153] and I was asked to talk on globalisation and the effects of globalisation, but also in the context of an agenda which was driven by theories and ideas of, in some sense, modernising India. I was forced to develop a theory of the discourse of modernity, the philosophical discourse of modernity. On this theory and understanding of modernity I saw it as characterised by five phases and each of the phases of modernity are associated with a big historical transformation, or potential transformation, and I will talk briefly about each of the five phases.[154]

---

152 2002 – From Science to Emancipation: Alienation and Enlightenment, New Delhi: Thousand Oaks & London: Sage. 2002 – Reflections on Meta-Reality: Transcendence, Emancipation and Everyday Life, New Delhi: Thousand Oaks & London: Sage 2002 – The Philosophy of Meta-Reality, Volume I: Meta-Reality: Creativity, Love and Freedom, New Delhi: Thousand Oaks & London: Sage. (Ed – There were a number of other books on metaReality planned but did not near completion).

153 So India acts as a stimulus to your bringing systematically together all the strands of the critique of the philosophical discourse of modernity you had been developing from the outset of your career. But it also brings you to see things you had not seen before. You now see the need to put it in a much bigger picture. Hartwig in Bhaskar, R & Hartwig M. (2010: 169)

154 (Ed) For a more detailed discussion see Hartwig M (2011) Bhaskar's Critique of the Philosophical Discourse of Modernity (https://goo.gl/GdRtA6 - checked 11/10/2016)

The Discourse of Modernity

Of course modernity is strongly associated with two other big developments: eurocentricity and capitalism. These three ideologies arose at roughly the same time and whereas the economist may focus on capitalism, it is convenient for philosophers to look at notions of modernity, bearing in mind a capitalist and eurocentric context of these ideas. What is conceptually characteristic of modernity is a couple formed by atomistic egocentricity and abstract universality. The atomistic egocentricity places the ego, which is devoid of all enduring characteristics, as in the subject pole, and the rest of the world is seen in terms of abstract universals not concrete universals.

There was an historical development at a conceptual level as well as an historical level in terms of institutions, and ways of interacting that is in terms of four-planer social being. Another way to look at the defining characteristic of conceptually modernity is to think about probably the most famous single saying in philosophy, which is Descartes: Cognito, ergo sum, which means of course, "I think, therefore I am". That is how he formulated the project of modern philosophy. When we think about this, when we look at it, "I think, therefore I am", we can see many of the characteristic errors and distortions of the discourse of modernity made out very clearly.

Thought is prior to being which means epistemology is prior to ontology, which is of course the epistemic fallacy. It is the thinking that is prioritised in a human being, not perhaps the emotions or the body; the human being is represented by thought. And then, "I think, therefore I am"; we have the priority of the I, the ego, over society in which the ego is born, even placed prior to the other human beings which were necessary conditions then, for their parents, the people who looked after them and raised them.

More generally of course this individualism there which scouts a principal which is essential to critical realist philosophy of social science, which is that you do not have an I, you do not have an agency unless you have a society, unless you have a social structure because the I who might want to speak must speak using a language which is something they do not create but something that is given to them and which they reproduce and transform.

So there is a very wrong individualism, prioritising individual over other individuals and over society and then of course over other species. This is very different from the world of pre-modernity. In the world of pre-modernity the peasants may have lived on the first floor of a building but the cattle and animals lived on the ground floor, and metaphorically they saw themselves as part of a chain of being stretching from perhaps inorganic beings through plants, animals, human beings to the enlightened ancestors to angels up to God or gods.[155]

Descartes on the other hand, and modernity generally, conceptualises the world in which there is man, and it is a tacitly gendered man, and the object of his manipulations which are not machines, so there is no differentiation between animals and machines.

---

155 See: Arthur O. Lovejoy (1976) The Great Chain of Being: A Study of the History of an Idea, Harvard University Press and E. M. W Tilyard (1998) The Elizabethan World, Pimlico

This is giving you the flavour of the origins of the philosophical discourse of modernity.

Now, in the five phases: the first form of this philosophical discourse is the *Classical Discourse of Modernity* and this is associated with the English Civil War, 1642-1651 and the English Revolution 1640-1660 and the French Revolution of 1789, the American Declaration of Independence, 1776.

Then the next phase of the discourse of modernity, which I sketch out more fully of course in Reflections on MetaReality[156] can be called *High Modernism*. This is the world of Proust and Freud and also Marx and the number of pivotal events, the failed revolutions of 1848 and then later in the 19th Century up to the Russian Revolution of 1917.

The third phase of modernity, and also the discourse of modernity, is associated particularly with what was called the *Theory of Modernisation*, and this arose in the wake of the defeat of fascism in 1945, the Indian Independence, but also partitioning of 1947 and the Chinese Revolution of 1949. The kind of writings associated with it might be Rostow's theories of growth,[157] the idea being, that modernity's history developed in a unilateral way, unilinear way. All societies must eventually get to the point that the leading nation is in, and of course, in the twentieth century, the leading nation was the United States and this is still a problem kind of phase and moment in the discourse of modernity.

---

156 See Bhaskar (2012c) Chapter One: Critical Realism: Beyond Modernism and Post-modernism. Also see: Bhaskar (2016: 177 - 184)

157 W.W. Rostow (1990) The Stages of Economic Growth: A Non-Communist Manifesto

The fourth phase is *Post-Modernism* and I see this very much as a form of the discourse of modernity. This is associated with the events of 1968 and the revolt of students and youth and the new social movements are closely associated with this.

Then the fifth form of discourse I have called *Bourgeois Triumphalism*, this is associated with the defeat or demise of the Soviet Union and the Soviet block in 1989-1991. The idea now is that the superiority of Western society has been clearly established and there is no need for any more big changes of any sort. This is the doctrine of Fukuyama[158] and reverberates in accord with the ending of history that Hegel foresaw, and claims in fact that had been achieved in the Prussia of his day. Of course, we do know, like all such claims of endings that it is wrong because you have 9/11; 2002 the onset of the war of terror; 2007-08 economic financial crisis of a very severe kind. All this suggests that perhaps we may be entering a sixth phase, which would be characterised by a new multi-polarity.

In 1989 for ten years or so there was a supremely hegemonic power USA, and with the rise of the so-called BRIC countries - Brazil, Russia, India, China, and other new newly emerging centres of power, there are a number of different models and poles of development and organisation. Socialism may be on the ropes in Europe but there are forms of socialism strongly developing in Latin America, for instance.

Be that as it may, critical realism has developed in its critique of the discourse of modernity and we argue that modernity has given us one

---

158 Francis Fukuyama (1992) The End of History and the Last Man

142

thing which is very important, and so it is not just be an aberration or a bad development, and that is the concrete singular, the individual self. This is a true gain of modernity that of course it has resulted in many oppressive developments that critical realism would want to critique and replace. So that is roughly the philosophical context in relation to which critical realism and the latest phase of philosophy metaReality developed.

Classical Modernism	Associated with the revolutionary moments of the English Civil War (1640-60), the American Declaration of Independence (1776) and the French Revolution (1789).
High Modernism	Associated with the revolutionary moments of 1848 in Europe and 1917 in Russia.
The theory of Modernisation	Associated with the moments of 1945 (the end of the Second World War and the defeat of fascism), 1947 (the Independence and Partition of India) and 1949 (the Chinese Revolution).
Postmodernism	Associated with the events of 1968 and the early 1970s, together with the rise of the 'new social movements'.
Bourgeois Triumphalism	Associated with the upheavals of 1989-1991 (the collapse of Soviet-style communism) and capitalist globalisation.

5.1 First sub-phase of globalisation lasts until 9/11 (2001).
5.2 Second sub-phase of the 'war on terror' ends with the credit crunch of 2007-08.
5.3 Third sub-phase of global multi-polarity (associated with the accelerated rise of the BRIC countries) and intensified and concatenated crisis.

Table Ten: The Five Stages of The Discourse of Modernity

The Holy Trinity[159] and Ecology

Just before metaReality developed, I wrote From East to West[160] and this scandalised most of my fellow critical realists by talking about religious themes and spirituality,[161] the philosophy of metaReality is secular but maintains some of what was established in From East to West: transcendental dialectical critical realism, about religion, which I briefly want to talk about. What it does is it invokes what I call the holy trinity of Basic Critical Realism.

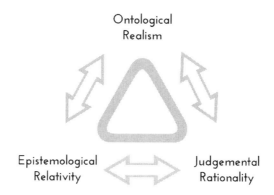

Figure Twelve: The Holy Trinity/Critical Realism Fulcrum

Which is situated as a context for talking about religion and particularly comparative religion. We can see the different religions as being attempts to characterise the absolute in different ways. Of course, different interpretations of a particular religion, like Christianity,

159 (Ed)Wilkinson M (2015) interestingly moves away from the use of "Holy Trinity" as perhaps being too Christian centric and suggests that a more appropriate term would be "Critical Realism Fulcrum".

160 Bhaskar (2015 Second Edition) From East To West: Odyssey of a Soul, Routledge

161 See Creaven S (2009)

Catholicism, Protestantism, etc, are precisely that: different interpretations of the tradition inaugurated by Jesus Christ. So this framework now is pretty widely accepted for understanding religion and religious education and that is a very positive gain, I think.[162]

I was at pains to distinguish spirituality from religion and I saw spirituality as a characteristic not only of religious projects but also of all great emancipatory projects. Then by the time the metaReality books were written I saw it as characteristic of everyday life, this metaReal level was a level of spirituality within our social ontology. I have not really got enough time to say much more about it but taking up now the points I made at the end of the first section about the extension of the dialectic of freedom[163] and the deepening social ontology. We can think briefly about what metaReality would have to say about the crises on all four-planes of contemporary social being, so what sort of resources could metaReality bring to bear.

Now if you take the level of the social structure, remember the four planes: material transactions with nature, social interactions between people, social structure, and the stratification of the embodied personality.

Let us have a look at social structure first, well, economic crisis so we have a fiscal financial crisis, it is arguable that what needs to happen is money and the financial structures need to be re-embedded within what

---

162 Archer, M, Collier A, Douglas, Porpora D (2004) and Wilkinson M (2015)

163 The dialectic of freedom reflects both, pursuing a path to eudaimonia that both treats everyone the same (reflecting universal humanity) and treats everyone as different (reflecting particular singularity). Thus, the end state is one in which the full freedom of each, reflecting singularity, is a condition of the full freedom of all, reflecting equality. Norrie A. (2010: 222)

could be called the real economy of people working and producing goods and services which are valued by other people. That real economy has to be re-embedded within its social pre-suppositions, that is, it has to be re-embedded and democratised within the social structure. Further, that society, and the social political structure, has to be re-embedded within the spirituality, which underpins it. And so this gives us a striking vision of going down to the ground state and the metaReal level as the way we want to travel in tackling the problems at the level of the social structure.

If we look at ecology, another huge source of crisis, at the level of material transactions with nature, I think it is absolutely unarguable that what we need is, from the point of view of the climate as a whole, less growth, that is degrowth, [164] and degrowth coupled with a radical redistribution of income. In fact, it is probably only the very well off who would be suffering any fall in their actual standard of material income. This combination of degrowth, this idea of degrowth, would be associated with the idea of a simplification of social existence.

We might think of all the things that we do not do: if you think about it, I know some of my friends in Australia and the States are listening and some will come to the conference which we are holding in a couple of weeks,[165] and that is really great. But do we need to actually go to Australia to experience it? We can see it on film, on video, we can talk

---

164 (Ed) For more on degrowth see: Bhaskar R, Naess P, Høyer K (2011) Chapter 14: From ecophilosophy to degrowth

165 (Ed) One of the aims of the streamed talks was to promote the 2014 International Conference for Critical Realism that was held in London over the summer of 2014.

to our Australian friends and we can phone them, Skype with them, we can also imagine, creatively visualise what that would be like.

Do we need to go to the Grand Canyon physically? I think not and I think that what we would be doing is developing capacities that we have of creative visualisation and communication that we have got lazy about developing. This would be sort of interior growth, simplification and shedding, these are things which would be associated with the basic model of the self that metaReality puts forward. Because metaReality is not saying that you have to become something radically different from what you are, metaReality is saying you are what you are and what you are is great,[166] but you are also a lot of other things and that is what you have to shed.

I mean, of course, this is maybe culturally a very difficult thing to implement, this regime of shedding[167] and degrowth, and of course we are only arguing that is should happen together with the huge re-distribution of resources, wealth and opportunities in a far more egalitarian direction.

---

166 [...] ultimately human beings are fine, they are absolutely fine, there is nothing wrong with them, they are beautiful. Even in their individuality; especially in their individuality for no two human beings are the same. We all have a unique dharma; we are all very special. But we are all absolutely fine. Some people have even said that we are all enlightened already. It is only this mess that we have on top of it which stops us from realising our enlightenment. Bhaskar in Scott D (2015: 50)

167 So what we are concerned with here is the articulation of ways of transforming our transformative praxis in the world. This is to initiate a programme of what we could call 'inner-work', that is of working in, as distinct from but also including the familiar concept of the physical work-out. Bhaskar (2012b: 153)

Just briefly, to look at the sort of metaReality in the plane of interactions: yes, we do understand, we have to understand the other, but of course we can deepen our understanding of the other through the practice of empathy, which I will come on to when I talk about conflict resolution.

Then there is the stratification of the embodied personality. What we would be seeking here is new levels and forms of integration that place the ground state in the centre of the self and allow us to work around and gradually get rid of all the non ground state things, and so become more efficient agents for our own wellbeing and the wellbeing of all.

Conflict Resolution and Peace

I want to say something about conflict resolution and peace. MetaReality puts forward two axioms or principles: the first is the principle of **Universal Solidarity** and this says that anyone can, in principle, understand anyone else. Second principle is **Axial Rationality**,[168] which says that in relation to any inter-human conflict there is always an optimal solution, which can be arrived at. Let me motivate the principle of Universal Solidarity a bit.

---

168 (in my recent, not yet fully published, work). *[The work was to be called Understanding, Peace and Security]* I argue that axial rationality stands alongside universal solidarity as a principle or presupposition which can be appealed to in the rational resolution of conflicts, especially those which seem to involve scientific (disciplinary, professional) cultural or moral incommensurability. People everywhere learn how to cook, drive cars, handle guns and use computers – this is a learning, which depends on our capacity to identify and correct mistakes. From this we can derive a basic universal principle of critique and self-critique, which, when coupled with the presupposition of universal solidarity, stating that we can in principle identify with any other human being, a principle which can be motivated, and transcendentally established, by the fact that we could have been them, gives us an organon or procedure for carrying out the basic critical realist theorem of judgemental rationality. However, this basis, deriving from the practical order, is learned, and is always in a social context, historically relevant and shifting – it is both transitive and always socially and culturally conditioned, contextualised and mediated; it is not 'foundationalist'. Furthermore, I would argue that, though we are born with certain innate capacities and infinite possibilities into a world of infinite possibilities, we always come into the world with a concretely singularised endowment and into concretely singularised circumstances – capacities and circumstances which at once constrain us and enable us to transcend these constraints. Moreover, we are born as dependent needy beings, dependent upon a context for our physical survival and the acquisition of the practical skills [...]Bhaskar in Bhaskar R & Hartwig M (2010: 80)

Universal Solidarity

What it says is you can in principle understand anyone else, even if you vehemently disagree or dislike them. If you think about it, if you have an enemy, what you have need to manipulate your life in the best possible way in relation to the enemies, what you need is the information about them with intelligence. You may know what they are thinking, what they are planning, what they are doing. So, arguably, it was this superior intelligence of the allies in the Second World War that eventually allowed them to establish a victory. This is say that in principle you ought to be able to understand Hitler, even though you completely abhor everything he does. And understanding Hitler in fact would be strategically and tactically the best way of dealing with him. So we should not demonise the terrorist, forget about them, what we have to do is understand them, understand why they are terrorists, why they feel that way, that is a principle of social science.

Now, of course we find it very difficult to understand many other people, particularly people from different cultures with different norms to ourselves. So, let me try and justify it by a thought experiment, what I would like you to do is to go back in your thought to the day you were born and imagine the day before, your parents had taken a trip from England, or from New England or from California, or New South Wales, wherever you are, or were born, to somewhere very different – Saudi Arabia or Japan, you would have grown up as a very different person. You would have spoken a different language, as effortlessly as you speak English now, or whatever language you do speak. You would have worn different clothes, played different games and had many different beliefs.

And even if as a result of processes of rational argument or persuasion you came to exactly the same beliefs as you have now, you would have come to them by a very different route. And what I suggest this experiment proves is that we can become one with very different people, a people who are very different from ourselves. We can become one with the others, with the other. That is Universal Solidarity.

Axial Rationality

Axial Rationality is established or begins to be justified by realising that we all live in a material object world; there are certain things that we all have to do to survive. We have to cook, we have to feed our children and when they grow up they will learn how to use computers and send emails but they can also learn how to use rifles and firearms. It is an extraordinary thing, you do not have societies that cannot fire rifles or cannot use emails, and these things are not obvious. In every society I claim there is, there has to be a process of learning involving critique and self-correction. That must be present in all societies. And that gives you resource for criticising self-criticism, or for criticising and transformatively developing your own society. These two principles are very important when it comes to conflict resolution.[169]

---

169 It is important to pursue axial-rationality because if we can show arguments why unity is basic and more important for social life than split, then we might expect to find something like a logic for resolving conflicts, which is a current topic of the critical realist philosophical project. In this manner, PMR claims that it has a logic for conflict resolution. This is fundamentally a logic for resolving antagonism since this argument emphasizes the notion that our human species is bounded by these two principles or transcendental capacities to identify with other fellow beings,

151

The most important thing to understand about the one you are having conflict with is that they are a human being, pretty much like you. So, in the case of military conflict wars are fought with the other given a non-human name like "Jerry" or "Uniform" or "Frog" because the truth that they are a human being like you is in a way too terrible to take on board.

This is the first thing one has to do in moving towards any peace negotiations is to understand the other as like oneself. Then, eventually, you will understand the other and yourself in a situation or relationship, transcendental identification working on common projects and then ultimately you will see the other as indeed part of yourself.

Eventually you will see the other and you will be able to look back on your experience of the other as being a part of yourself that you had not developed, a part of yourself that you had not recognised and that would be a tremendously liberating and the de-alienating moment for yourself and your other.[170]

---

which is based on P1: universal solidarity and P2: axial-rationality, and thus identify, recognize and reconcile with others. Nunez I (2013: 95)

170 We become one with the other, not in order necessarily to agree with the other or to be the other permanently; but in order to eliminate the other. So we have to understand what are the blocks, the constraints, the checks on our own emancipation, what are the blocks, the constraints, the checks on the emancipation of all people, all beings everywhere. We have to become one with them. We have to totally understand them to eliminate them, that is these blocks, constraints, forces. This means that the spiritual being is also a warrior, but he is a warrior at peace with himself. Bhaskar (2011: 315)

Learning[171]

In the case of learning, this is very interesting. Let me first of all relate learning to emancipation. There is something that is very important to understand which is that you cannot emancipate anyone else. At the end of the day, emancipation is always self-emancipation. You can go to a prison, unlock all the doors but eventually the prisoner has to come out. Of course, you can help and aid that process of emancipation, but the last step has to be taken by person who would be emancipated, or is to be emancipated.[172]

In exactly the same way I could say you cannot teach anyone but yourself because I could put on the whiteboard or blackboard a logical theorem which attempts to show how if P implies Q and if you have P and Q then you can say, if P then Q. But of course if you do not understand that, if you do not see how that works, then that is absolutely useless. I could put another logical theorem on the board and if you do

---

171 *(Ed) I would highly recommend Professor David Scott's book Roy Bhaskar: A Theory of Education –* "This book has a highly unusual form. The first and last chapters bracket the main body of the text, which consists of transcriptions of two interviews with Roy, the text of a research proposal that we jointly worked on, and a transcription of a lecture Roy gave in India in 2002 specifically about education. The original intention was that the major part of the book would consist of four long interviews with Roy, but his death intervened before the interviews could be completed". Scott D (2015) Roy Bhaskar: A Theory of Education, Springer.

172 What I want to say is that the project of education, the project of enlightenment , and the project of universal self-realisation are the same, or all turn on a single matter, and this turns on eliminating the heteronomy, eliminating everything which is not essentially you. And in that process of eliminating everything which is not essentially you, you will automatically be working towards the elimination of everything which is not essentially everyone else. Bhaskar (2011: 305)

not get that then it is like Wittgenstein says – mathematics cannot come and grab you by the throat, you have to understand it. There has to be that eureka, that aha moment, that now I see it moment, and that is what the educator, that is what the teacher is always working towards.[173]

Well, if you look at a typical learning of something, whether it is a language like French or a skill like riding a bicycle you can make out various phases.[174] The first phase is when you cannot do it and when you get on the bike, you fall off. Then comes that aha, or I see it or I get, when you can stay on the bike for a bit, or you can speak one or two sentences of French.

Then comes the interesting phase when you are learning how to ride a bike or you learn how to ride it in different conditions, or if it is a car then you are learning how to drive a car, and you learn which way you have to turn the wheel when you are reversing, how to do hill starts

---

173 You have to say for example, if P implies Q, and P then Q; and P therefore (because if P implies Q and P then Q) Q. Does this help? So what is the condition of this, it is an extraordinary condition. The condition is it means they must already know it. Because if it comes from within they must already have the knowledge and this is in fact nothing other than Plato's theory that all education is anamnesis, that what you are doing is bringing out something that was implicit, enfolded, potential within them, you are actualising it, making it explicit, but unless it was there, you could not have that 'ah', that 'I see it', that coming together when the pupil understands what the teacher is trying to say. So the primacy of the standpoint of self-referentiality is not only important for emancipation, it is just as important for education, which is our main theme today. Bhaskar (2012a: 302)

174 (Ed) In May 2016, I gave a presentation on education, creativity, and metaReality for the University College London Institute of Education's critical realism reading group. The presentation explores in more detail that which Roy covers in this section. A version of the presentation can be found at https://goo.gl/WipMO4

and what to do when the roads are icy, etc. Then, eventually you get to a point magical when you can just do it, and this whole process of metaReality describes as unfolding the enfolded, because you have that within you, that possibility of speaking French or riding a bike, or knowing how to drive, within you.

The process of education, of learning, is a process of your unfolding under the best possible conditions, ideally, the implicit knowledge that you have. This brings to education something of a platonic element.

Plato had the theory of amenesis, which was a theory that we have to un-forget in order to know something. And metaReality is not arguing that you do actually know how to speak French, if you do not, all it is saying at a very learner-centred philosophical approach, that you have the potential to speak French and the process of education is the process of unfolding that capacity which you have, that possibility.

And these different stages of a typical dialectic of learning correspond to stages of creation,[175] and the first stage is the stage in which you decide that you want to do something and that is called, traditionally, the **Circle of Calling**. The second stage in which I see it is called the **Cycle of Creativity**, proper.

The third stage is the **Cycle of Formation**. The fourth stage is the **Cycle of Making,** when you can actually do things without thinking about them.

---

175 See Bhaskar (2012b 115-117)

You see the third stage, the level of formation, your head is full of a whole lot of rules, how I construct the sentence in French I have to do this, that and the other, or when I reverse a car I have to do X, Y, Z, and the fourth stage, when you can just do things spontaneously, the knowledge is inbuilt, it is part of your being, it is not rattling around in your head.

Then the fifth stage, the **Circle of Reflection**, is seeing your intentionality as reflected in the world,[176] where you have actually driven all the way to, I do not know, New York or San Francisco or Sydney, or wherever, and you have actually written a letter in French, or you have actually sent an email, or fired a rifle in the air for that matter, your intentionality is being reflected.

---

176 These five cycles or circles of creation correspond to, first, the initial impulse—traditionally called the 'word' or 'calling', or the lightening flash or emanation, the creator's will to impose on the world. The second is creation proper itself, the articulation and emergence, de novo, of something which had never existed before. The third cycle is that of formation—this is the shaping or binding, the activity or labour of love, desire or worth in which the imaginative creative impulse of thought is now shaped into an object about to be released onto the world. This is the circle of formation. Then there is the circle of making, its physical objectification, the manifestation of the initial impulse or intentionality of the creator. Each of these cycles presupposes the prior ones. Finally there is the circle of reflection, or reflexivity, which corresponds to a moment of self-consciousness or return (namely of the result or consequence of his objectification) to the creator/maker. Bhaskar (2012b: 108)

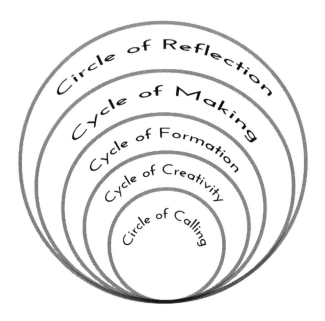

Figure Thirteen: The Circles of Creation

So, I'm going to have to wind up now because I think we are going to be moved from this room. I would like to have said something about the limitations of the discursive intellect; the intellect, which is concerned with thinking, because thinking virtually never, takes you to the solution.

It is a necessary condition for it, go through all the possibilities, but what happens when you arrive at the solution of a problem is you arrive by the action of another part of your mind or consciousness, which is above, beyond or beneath thought; sometimes in the West it is called the unconscious, the unconscious clearly comes into it, it could also be seen as supramental consciousness, it comes from un-thought.

This is a topic, however, that I suggest, if you want to follow it up, you read *From Science to Emancipation,* [177] or *The Philosophy of metaReality,* [178] and then I have not time for the most wonderful topic of all, which is a topic of love. [179][180]

---

177 See Bhaskar (2012a) Chapter 12 The Limits of Thought.

178 See Bhaskar (2012b) Chapter Three: The Zen of Creativity and the Critique of the Discursive Intellect, Section 6: Creativity and the Limits of Thought

179 See Bhaskar (2012b) Chapter Four The Tao of Love and Unconditionality in Commitment.

180 See Bhaskar (2012a) Chapter 13 Unconditionality in Love

The vision of metaReality is very much that love is the cement of the universe, that love is the great binding force. When we are loving someone, love is their ground state.

And then we have ground state loving ground state. Then we have love, loving, love, and love can love love in ever widening circle.[181] So, having said that, just add the important point that love is not a form of behaviour, its not saying love everyone, does not mean sleep with everyone, for instance.

It does not mean hug everyone; it means that you treat each person according to what their higher self would want.[182]

---

181 (Ed) The metaReality five circles of Love are (1) love of oneself – this should be of one's ground state and of those elements within one's embodied personality consistent with it; (2) love of another human being – if the love is from the ground state and reciprocated, then we have the situation of 'love loving love'; (3) love of all human beings – through generalised co-presence, aspiring to universal self-realisation;(4) love of all beings; and (5) love of god, the cosmic envelope or the totality.

182 See Gunnarsson L (2014) The Contradictions of Love: Towards a feminist-realist ontology of sociosexuality Routledge

"Love is the totalising, binding, unifying, healing force in the universe. And, just in virtue of there being a 'universe' (oneverse), it is the most powerful force in being. Fear, and all the other negative emotions, depend on the absence or incompleteness of love. Thus the negative emotions, such as greed and anger, all depend on self-alienation, an alienation of self from Self, of personality from alethic truth."

Roy Bhaskar (2012b: 175) The Philosophy of metaReality: Creativity, Love and Freedom

"Transcendence is alive, as experience, and present everywhere."

Roy Bhaskar (2012a: 49).

Afterword

Donald Clark

Critical realism came into my life at an interesting and turbulent time. I had been searching for some framework with which I could make sense of the world, my place in it, and the questions that inquisitive restless minds often engage with: What is life? What is reality? What is love? What is intelligence, creativity and joy? Essentially, what is it to be a human and to live in this world, this universe?

I often found frustration in that a concept or framework is really just somebody's lens into his or her own limited reality! It was enough to borrow such insights from time to time but ultimately I thought with so many differing lenses how could one make sense of anything from so many singular perspectives! I engaged with so many narratives and not one defining truth could be teased out from these stories, played repeatedly throughout cultures and histories, so it was at a point of great nihilism that I found Critical Realism.

I remember one day sitting down whilst having the privilege to be with Roy's voice and physical presence. I was listening to Roy speak about the theory of metaReality and remember seeing one of his books on a table that had the tenants *"Love, Will, Creativity and Freedom"* written on the front cover!

As he spoke I noticed how these tenants, these simple words started to shine a truth, I started to ask myself questions! How do we embody those essential qualities, how do we let go of our identity enough to open up into something larger and more profound than us?

In that moment I realised how Roy was fiercely engaging the study of ontology and privileging it over our seductive relationship with epistemology; a relationship that has been unwrapping itself with us for millennia.

I realised Critical Realism was not just a theory; in fact it would be hard for me to reduce or describe it in such terms. I had woken to the simplicity of Roy's very complex work, a work he had been grappling with most of his adult years, ...suddenly the words struck me "what is real" and how do we come to know what is real; how do find this out?

Roy had built up a series of thought experiments and philosophical inquiries that would allow one to engage the real and to even tease it from its narrative!

This was not a theory but more a study of truth stripped from the epistemic engagement we hold onto dearly, in the same way that the scientific method is not really a theory but an engagement with a process. So too is Roy's work with truth, only this time and unlike science we are not attempting to build high castles of related knowledge we are attempting to strip those things away, to see what is fundamental to the narratives we walk and live in. And so we return to Love, Freedom, Will, and Creativity!

If we begin here, we have the story of the universe unfolding with us and out of us. It was through the many hours of conversation with Gary and simply just being in Roy's presence hearing him talk that slowly, the thoughts and insights developed over a lifetime of research began to find its way into my being and express itself through me.

Roy once said we must do our work, it is not enough to be fed, to be happy, to be content, and to live with our needs met. There is a need that will gnaw at us for a lifetime; it is the work we have come to do in the world.

I believe this book is a legacy of Roy's work and Gary's embodiment of his vision, I believe that in his words Roy's spirit lives on. It is a strong and loving spirit! I only knew Roy for a short time but he affected me, he moved me, his words, his character, and the relationships I enjoy are in part Roy's own legacy. Roy lives on through me, and all the others he has encountered.

We live in complex and uncertain times. At the core of Roy's work is an engagement with the real. To engage in this way is to live with uncertainty, to live in it, to move past fear, and to be grounded in love. It is from this place that we can see and live the possible potentials that are gifted us that our lives matter, that we can make change happen.

It is my hope that this book shows you that truth is transformation and that engaging with the real is an engagement with the process that holds life together.

"The way to be a good social agent is to be in touch with and informed by your ground-state; you cannot then be oblivious to structural sin and ecological degradation, you must be an active agent involved in remedying them."

Roy Bhaskar (2010: 215) The Formation of Critical Realism: A Personal Perspective.

Bibliography

Alderson, P. 2013. *Childhoods Real and Imagined: Volume 1: An introduction to critical realism and childhood studies* (Ontological Explorations) Routledge

Archer, M, Collier A, Douglas, Porpora, D. 2004. *Transcendence Critical realism and God*, Routledge,

Baggini, J & Fosl, P. 2010. *The Philosopher's Toolkit: a compendium of philosophical concepts and methods* Blackwell Publishing Ltd

Bhaskar, R. 2008a. *A Realist Theory of Science.* London: Routledge

Bhaskar, R. 2008b. *Dialectic: The Pulse of Freedom.* London: Routledge

Bhaskar, R. 2009. *Scientific Realism and Human Emancipation.* London: Routledge

Bhaskar, R. 2010. *Plato Etc: Problems of Philosophy and Their Resolution*, London: Routledge

Bhaskar, R. 2012a. *From Science to Emancipation: Alienation and the Actuality of Enlightenment*, London: Routledge

Bhaskar, R. 2012b. *The Philosophy of metaReality: Creativity, Love and Freedom.* London: Routledge

Bhaskar, R. 2012c. *Reflections on metaReality: Transcendence, Emancipation and Everyday Life.* London: Routledge

Bhaskar, R. 2015 Fourth Edition. *The Possibility of Naturalism*, London: Routledge

Bhaskar, R. 2015 Second Edition. *From East To West: Odyssey of a Soul,* London: Routledge

Bhaskar, R. 2016. *Enlighten Common Sense: The Philosophy of Critical Realism.* London: Routledge.

Bhaskar, R & Danermark, B. 2006. *Metatheory, Interdisciplinarity and Disability Research: A Critical Realist Perspective,* Scandinavian Journal of Disability Research, 8:4, 278-297, http://dx.doi.org/10.1080/15017410600914329

Bhaskar, R & Hartwig, M. 2010. *The Formation of Critical Realism: A Personal Perspective.* London: Routledge,

Bhaskar, R, Cheryl Frank, C, Karl Georg Høyer, K, Næss, P, and Parker, J. (eds). 2010. *Interdisciplinarity and Climate Change.* London: Routledge

Bhaskar R, Naess P, Høyer, K. 2011 *Ecophilosophy in a World of Crisis: Critical realism and the Nordic Contributions,* London: Routledge

Bhaskar, R. 2013. 'Prolegomenon' in *Engaging with the World: Agency, Institutions, Historical Formation,* M. Archer and A. Maccarini (eds). London: Routledge

Bhaskar, R, 2014. "Introduction' in Edwards P K, & O'Mahoney J, & Vincent S. 2014. *Studying Organizations Using Critical Realism A Practical Guide.* OUP: Oxford

Bhaskar, R, Esbjörn-Hargens, S, Hedlund, N, Hartwig, M, 2016. *Metatheory for the Twenty-First Century: Critical Realism and Integral Theory in Dialogue,* London: Routledge

Bhaskar, M 2013. v12 The Place of Totality in Dialectical, Critical *Realism Journal of Critical Realism*

Cohnitz, D. & Rossberg, M. 2006 *Nelson Goodman,* Acumen

Collier, A. 1994. *An Introduction to Roy Bhaskar's Critical Realism*. London: Verso

Creaven, S. 2009. *Against the Spiritual Turn: Marxism, Realism, and Critical Theory*, London: Routledge

Edwards, P K, & O'Mahoney J, & Vincent, S. 2014 *Studying Organizations Using Critical Realism A Practical Guide* OUP Oxford

Fleetwood, S. & Hesketh A. 2010 *Explaining the Performance of Human Resource Management,* Cambridge University Press

Gunnarsson, L. 2014. *The Contradictions of Love: Towards a feminist-realist ontology of sociosexuality*, London: Routledge

Hartwig, M. (Ed) 2007. *Dictionary of Critical Realism*. London: Routledge

Hartwig, M & Morgan J (Ed) 2013. *Critical Realism and Spirituality,* London: Routlege

Hume, D, A Treatise of Human Nature, Vol. II (London: J. M. Dent, 1740/1934), Book II, Section III, 128

Irwin, L. 1997 The Web Site for Critical Realism WSCR Glossary – http://www.criticalrealism.com/glossary.php entry Transdictive Complex

Kuhn, T. 2012. *The Structure of Scientific Revolutions: 50th Anniversary Edition Paperback* University of Chicago Press

McWherter, D. 2013. *The Problem of Critical Ontology: Bhaskar Contra Kant*. London: Palgrave Macmillan

Norrie, A. 2010. *Dialectic and Difference: Dialectical Critical Realism and the Grounds of Justice*. London: Routledge

Nunez, I. 2014. *Critical Realist Activity Theory: An Engagement With Critical Realism and Cultural-Historical Activity Theory.* London: Routledge

Pilgrim, D. 2014. *Understanding Mental Health: A critical realist exploration,* London: Routledge

Price, L. 2007. "*Critical Realist versus Mainstream Interdisciplinarity.*"Journal of Critical Realism 2014; 13(1), 52-76.

Proudfoot M, & Lacey AR. 2009. *The Routledge Dictionary of Philosophy,* Routledge

Robinson, A. 2014. An A to Z of Theory | Alain Badiou: The Event https://ceasefiremagazine.co.uk/alain-badiou-event/

Scott, D. 2015. *Roy Bhaskar: A Theory of Education* Springer

Seo, M. 2014. *Reality and Self-Realization: Bhaskar's Metaphilosophical Journey Toward Non-Dual Emancipation,* London: Routledge

Taft, M. W. 2014. *Nondualism: A Brief History of a Timeless Concept.* Cephalopod Rex

Wilkinson, M. 2015. *A Fresh Look at Islam in a Multi-Faith World: a philosophy for success through education,* London: Routledge

Bibliography

A Brief Introduction to the Philosophy of metaReality

Archer, M S, Collier, A, Porpora, D V (2014). *Transcendence: Critical Realism and God*. London: Routledge

Bhaskar, R. 2008a. *A Realist Theory of Science*. London: Routledge

Bhaskar, R. 2008b. *Dialectic: The Pulse of Freedom*. London: Routledge

Bhaskar, R. 2012a. *From Science to Emancipation: Alienation and the Actuality of Enlightenment,* Reprint Routledge

Bhaskar, R. 2012b. *The Philosophy of metaReality: creativity, love and freedom,* London Routledge

Bhaskar, R. 2012c. *Reflections on metaReality: Transcendence, Emancipation and Everyday Life*. London Routledge

Bhaskar, R. 2015 Fourth Edition. *The Possibility of Naturalism*, London: Routledge

Creaven, S, 2011. *Against the Spiritual Turn: Marxism, Realism, and Critical Theory*, London: Routledge

Gilbert, E. (Ed) 2011. *Conversations in Non Duality: Twenty Six Awakenings*, Conscious.tv

Seo, M. 2014. *Reality and Self-Realization: Bhaskar's Metaphilosophical Journey Toward Non-Dual Emancipation*, London: Routledge

Shun'Ei, T. 2009. *Living Yogacara: An Introduction to Consciousness*, US: Wisdom Publications

Wilkinson, M. 2015. *A Fresh Look at Islam in a Multi-Faith World: a philosophy for success through education*, London: Routledge

Printed in Great Britain
by Amazon